THE ULTIMATE CAREER COACH

Faith In Finding Your Dream Job

George Goodwyn Jr.

WESTBOW
PRESS®
A DIVISION OF THOMAS NELSON
& ZONDERVAN

WestBow Press books may be ordered through booksellers or by contacting:

WestBow Press
A Division of Thomas Nelson & Zondervan
1663 Liberty Drive
Bloomington, IN 47403
www.westbowpress.com
844-714-3454

ISBN: 978-1-6642-8848-5 (sc)
ISBN: 978-1-6642-8847-8 (e)

Print information available on the last page.

WestBow Press rev. date: 7/31/2023

To my wife, Sarah, my first co-leader in our Church of the Highlands small group, Faith to Find a Job

To my pastor, Chris Erwin, who encouraged me to start the small group in the first place

To all the co-leaders over the years who have volunteered their time and energy to help others find jobs: Nick Pincumbe, Jim Hawk, James Hawk, Chad Bianchi, Conwell Hooper, Kimber Khouri, Joyce Robinson, Beth Sorrells, Tom Methvin and Dee Cook

And lastly to my Ultimate Career Coach, our heavenly Father, who wants the absolute eternal best for all of us

CONTENTS

PREFACE

Around 2012, I was looking to fill some positions at our homebuilding company, and the unemployment rate in the United States was still suffering from the last recession. As I was searching for a way to fill these positions, I came across a computer program a church could attach to their website that would connect church members looking for employment with those who had positions to fill. This could be done all online and what I thought would be less cumbersome.

I went to my local campus pastor, Chris Erwin, and asked if the Church of The Highlands would consider putting this computer program on their website. Before I could finish, he immediately responded, "Sounds like a small group." Now the last thing I wanted to do was lead a job seekers' small group. In fact, I was looking for a way to hire people with as little conversation as possible.

After praying about it for several months, my wife and I launched a small group, Faith to Find a Job, based on a book written by L. C. Brown Bush. Great book, by the way. And we started to have people sign up for the small group.

When we started, we expected to have young individuals looking to start their real first job and thought we could help them along the way. But we found out that our group attracted middle-aged men and women either stuck in what they thought was a dead-end job or had been let go for a variety of reasons.

During those early years of the group, we followed the outline of Ms. Brown's book: filling out applications, writing resumes, and searching the internet for jobs. All of those steps are important, but we found that a simple biblical process obtained greater results.

1. Write down what you want your dream job to look like.
2. Pray about it.
3. Have others pray in agreement.
4. Pray for others as well to get their dream jobs.
5. Remove whatever obstacle is standing in the way of God's miracle.

Since we have adopted these steps, we have seen many individuals get a new job that was better than what we were praying for.

We hope this small book will help you draw closer to the Lord, our Ultimate Career Coach, as well as seek Him for wisdom and guidance. As a result, we hope you will find your dream job so you can make a greater eternal impact. We want you to have the best job possible so you can be all the Lord created you to be.

1

INTRODUCTION

* * * * * * * * *

Your work is going to fill a large part of your life, and the only way to be truly satisfied is to do what you believe is great work. And the only way to do great work is to love what you do. If you haven't found it yet, keep looking. Don't settle. As with all matters of the heart, you'll know when you find it.

—Steve Jobs

Obviously Steve Jobs made an incredible impact at Apple and on the world as a whole. I confess I don't know much about him, and I suspect twenty years from now, most will not even recognize the name. However, this statement is right about the job you have or the one you want.

As an adult, we will spend almost a third of our life at work and getting to and from work. From my experience, most people are not satisfied, pleased, or happy with their job and where they work. I would go so far as to say that most people don't enjoy what they do. I personally don't know many who jump out of bed every morning and can't wait for the day to begin so they can get to work. I know these people exist. My pastor is one of those individuals. But those who get excited about what is in store for the day make an incredible impact on those around them. We read about these people, see them on TV, and wonder how they could be so excited about the opportunities they face every day. As Steve Jobs says, you ought to "love what you do."

I would love to wake up every morning excited about the day. I would love to be passionate about most of what I do. I would love to know that what I do makes a real lasting difference. I would love to leave a legacy that really matters. I would love to love what I do.

I have been a homebuilder for over thirty years. I don't love it. I am good at it. But I don't love it. Many times, I have wanted to do something else. I have even pursued other career opportunities, only to come back to homebuilding because it is what I know and what I have been successful at. The problem is me. What is wrong with me? We live in the greatest country ever to exist on this planet. 99.9 percent of the world wish and pray that they could be in my shoes.

So the problem must be me. How do I change my perspective and attitude? How do I change my heart? Maybe I can't do any of this on my own. I need help. I need supernatural help to change my attitude, perspective, and heart. If these changes could occur, I would have more joy, purpose, and direction and leave an eternal legacy.

Even though I am sixty-two, I am determined to have these changes occur. I want these changes to happen for you as well. When these changes occur, they will impact our home and work life. Both of these are so intertwined. Neither aspect can be really successful unless both are in harmony.

I believe Steve Jobs had it right when he said, "As with all matters of the heart, you'll know when you find it." I submit that *"it"* is Jesus. If the *"it"* is not Jesus, most everything is done in vain. If the *"it"* is missing, you know it. There is a hole inside of you that you can feel. What you have done or will accomplish will have no real positive eternal impact, and your relationships will not be there best.

Therefore, I believe the change I need starts with Jesus. Everyone can make a lasting, eternal impact wherever they are and at whatever they do. Everyone can have a different perspective about their day if they look forward to being a part of God's plan to point others toward Jesus.

The apostle Paul was a tent-maker. Every time he showed up in a new town, he would set up shop. He would work during the day making tents, hoping that God would lead lost people to him. I suspect Paul would stop what he was doing so he could share the truth about Jesus Christ. His profession was tent-making. His vocation and purpose were to be an example and to introduce others to Jesus.

I don't know this, and the Bible doesn't say anything about it, but I believe that Paul made great tents. I bet they were made right, he kept his word about his work, delivery schedule, and warranty. If he did all these things right, he would earn his customers' respect and confidence. He would have opened the door to being able to share the truth about his real purpose in life.

What would it look like if everything I did were so I could ultimately share the truth about Jesus with others? It wouldn't matter what I actually did. What would matter is how I did it. What would matter was my attitude while I did it. What would matter would be how I treated customers after the sale. What would matter is how I treat the people I work with, not just the customers.

My perspective and heart are not in the right place most of the time. I am tired—tired of people, problems, and the day-to-day routine. (Others pray to have my problems.) I am reminded of this verse where God responds to Jeremiah's complaints,

> **"If you have raced with men on foot and they have worn you out, how can you compete with horses? If you stumble in safe country, how will you manage in the thickets by the Jordan?"** (Jeremiah 12:5 NIV, for emphasis I have put everything God said in bold letters)

Are you feeling worn out? I know I feel worn out lots of times. The great Jeremiah felt worn out and complained to God about it. So you are not alone. And yet I want to run with the horses. I want to compete on a bigger stage. I think I can handle it. However, how can I do more and handle bigger challenges when I am stumbling in what is my comfort zone, the safe country?

Most people I know want better jobs, more responsibility, more authority (power), and more pay. More. More. More. I confess I want the same. How can I handle more when I am complaining, worn out, and stumbling where I am today?

How does someone change their perspective and ultimately their heart? When I put my selfish desires first above everything else, others second, and God third, I have everything upside down. When I flip these priorities, I stop complaining as much, gain energy, and stumble less. Could you do more when these priorities change? If we could just realize and remember that God is working everything out for our eternal best. "And we know that in all things God works for the good of those who love him, who have been called according to his purpose" (Romans 8:28 NIV).

And guess what? God wants to give us the ability, wisdom, direction, and purpose to accomplish great eternal work.

> And God is able to bless you abundantly, so that in all things at all times, having all that you need, you will abound in every good work. (2 Corinthians 9:8 NIV)

> Now to him who is able to do immeasurably more than all we ask or imagine, according to his power that is at work within us, to him be glory in the church and in Christ Jesus throughout all generations, for ever and ever! Amen. (Ephesians 3:20–21 NIV)

Jesus said, *"Ask and it will be given to you; seek and you will find; knock and the door will be opened to you. For everyone who asks receives; the one who seeks finds; and to the one who knocks, the door will be opened"* (Matthew 7:7–8 NIV, for emphasis I have put everything Jesus said in italics).

In the following chapters, I hope to make a case for how you can achieve what you would hope your full potential would be. However, I believe that God, the Ultimate Career Coach, can help you achieve "immeasurably more than all we ask or imagine." I believe, regardless of where you start, your present education, your race, your gender, or your history, God can take you to new heights and be eternally successful. He wants to make you a new creature:

> Therefore, if anyone is in Christ, the new creation has come: The old has gone, the new is here! All this is from God, who reconciled us to himself through Christ and gave us the ministry of reconciliation. (2 Corinthians 5:17–18 NIV)

> You were taught to leave your old self. This means that you must stop living the evil way you lived before. That old self gets worse and worse, because people are fooled by the evil they want to do. You must be made new in your heart and in your thinking. Be that new person who was made to be like God, truly good and pleasing to him. (Ephesians 4:22–24 Easy-To-Read Version)

I also believe that you can follow the outline of this book and get a better job, make more money, have more authority, and be more productive. However, until you settle the question of "Who do you say Jesus is?" you will never be all you were created to be. My hope is that you have settled this question once and for all. Nothing else really matters until you have claimed Jesus as your Savior and that you depend on Him.

So you next need to ask yourself: Do I want to be the best I can be? Am I capable of more? Can I do better? If you are reading this book, you have already answered these questions in the affirmative. You know there is more out there, you are capable of more, and you could do better. So the real and pressing question is, "What is holding you back?" Quit looking for excuses!

What is holding you back from pursuing Jesus?

What is holding you back from going all in?

What is holding you back from being all you were created to be?

Everyone has a ball and chain weighing them down. For some, it is the past. For others, it is an addiction. For others, it's fear. Only you know what is holding you back that you need to be set free from.

Satan came to kill, steal, and destroy. He wants you to be chained down and prevented from going all in. Jesus said, *"The thief* [Satan] *comes only to steal and kill and destroy; I have come that they may have life, and have it to the full"* (John 10:10 NIV).

Satan is trying to destroy you. If he can make you miserable and unproductive at work, he knows this will bleed over into the rest of your life. Studies show that those who are unhappy at work make less money and have more problems at home. Their health suffers. It only makes sense that if you are unhappy in the third of your life where you are supposed to be the most productive, the rest of your life will be infected. Satan and our minds trap us and hold us prisoner.

Getting set free is no easy task. The only way I know is to turn your life fully over to Jesus. He can change your direction, free you from the ball and chain, turn your life around, and put you on the path toward making an eternal difference.

Now in my experience, this doesn't happen overnight. This takes time, sometimes lots of time. We want everything yesterday. We are impatient. Finding a better job takes time. If you are not prepared to go the distance, you will never get to the finish line that God intended for you to reach.

Be patient. (I dislike this word.) It's a process. (I dislike it when people tell me this.) However, the Ultimate Career Coach wants to change you and shape you into a better you through the process. I can remember going to work on summer jobs, and after one week, I thought I could be the president of the company. I thought I could do this. I was so wrong. I look back and can't figure out how I even got this far. If not for Jesus, there is no telling how bad things would be.

All the following chapters are based on the Word of God, your Bible. All the principles in the Bible are still relevant today as they were when they were written. My hope is that if you have the guts to read the rest of this book, you will see how God wants to use you, and you will know He made you to make a real difference.

All it takes is a little faith to find a job and not just a better job, but your dream job. Faith the size of a mustard seed can make all the difference if you put your faith in Jesus and what God, your Ultimate Career Coach, can do. Just do your part!

2

WRITE IT DOWN

* * * * * * * * *

Isaac Newton's first law of motion (the law of inertia) states that an object at rest remains at rest and an object in motion remains in motion at a constant speed and in a straight line unless acted on by an unbalanced force. An object at rest remains at rest. A person at rest remains at rest. A stuck person tends to remain stuck.

We need an unbalanced force to start us in the right direction and get us moving. I believe in God's principle of writing it down. I believe that the way to start moving or get unstuck is to write out what our vision is or what we would hope to happen. This would be what we hope in our career, job, and/or business. This also applies to all of life: marriage, parenting, retirement, and so forth. What do you hope for?

When you ask a child what they want to be when they grow up, they quickly respond that they want to be a firefighter, doctor, or president. When you ask an adult, they typically have a hard time telling you. What I typically hear is, "I know what I think I want to happen. It is in my head, but I can't or haven't been able to put it into words." Or it may be that they are just scared to say it out loud to someone else because it seems so impossible.

God's Word says to start by writing it down.

And then God answered: **"Write this. Write what you see. Write it out in big block letters so that it can be read on the run. This vision-message is a witness pointing to what's coming. It aches for the coming— it can hardly wait! And it doesn't lie. If it seems slow in coming, wait. It's on its way. It will come right on time."** (Habakkuk 2:2–3 The Message)

What stops you from writing it down? Just because you think it is in your head, it is not enough. You need to make it more tangible. Writing it down is the first step of faith, especially if you believe that God's Word does not return void. God said, **"Write it out."**

Why? Because it is a witness of what God is going to do. **"It's on its way"** as soon as you start to write it out. **"It will come right on time."** When? When you are ready. When you have completed all your next steps. But that is in the future and in subsequent chapters. First and foremost, **"write it out."**

Be bold and courageous. Think big. We have a big God! Believe in the impossible because we have God who performs the impossible.

Writing it out is like planting a seed. For the farmer, this takes faith. He believes that if he does all he can do, God will grow the seed into a harvest.

All successful businesses have a written mission and vision statement. They have written out a one-year (short-term) and a five-year (longer-term) plan. Would you invest your money in a business with no vision, mission, or plan? Is it any different for you? How many people do you know who have these written down? Not many, I would guess. But of those that have written down their vision, I have seen God make things happen. They are moving in a positive direction far faster than you could have believed possible.

Also, don't complicate this step too much. Be specific but make it short and sweet. You want to be able to remember it when you pray or someone asks. You want to be able to read it on the run. Also, this vision will change over time, so don't get trapped into thinking somehow this is permanent. It's never too late to start. It's never too late to write it down. It's never too late to plant the seed.

In all these years of helping people find jobs, the ones that get the job quicker are the ones who have written down their dream or vision. In fact, they are the ones who get jobs better than they had hoped for. The Lord told Joshua and He is telling you as well:

> **"Keep this Book of the Law always on your lips; meditate on it day and night, so that you may be careful to do everything written in it. Then you will be prosperous and successful. Have I not commanded you? Be strong and courageous. Do not be afraid; do not be discouraged, for the LORD your God will be with you wherever you go."** (Joshua 1:8–9 NIV)

Do you want to be prosperous and successful? Do you want to be strong and courageous? I know these are dumb questions because if you are reading this, you have already answered them. But we all need to remember and know that **"the Lord your God will be with you wherever you go." "Meditate on it** [your vision and God's plan for your life] **day and night, so that you may be careful to do everything written in it** [the Bible]."

The first step to getting the best job and seeing your career jump started is to write it out. What is your vision? What do you want to do that will make a real difference? **"Write it out."**

> "Where there is no vision, the people perish: but he that keepeth the law, happy is he." (Proverbs 29:18 KJV).

> "Commit thy works unto the Lord, and thy thoughts shall be established." (Proverbs 16:1 KJV).

Your vision will change and should expand over time. We all know that change is inevitable. We need change. But you need a starting point. Once you have the starting point, you are in motion.

So back to Newton's first law of motion, an object in motion remains in motion at a constant speed and in a straight line unless acted on by an unbalanced force. Expect the unbalanced force. In fact, pray for it. We want God, the Ultimate Force, to act upon us and our vision.

> "Commit to the Lord whatever you do, and he will establish your plans." (Proverbs 16:3 NIV)

> "In their hearts humans plan their course, but the LORD establishes their steps." (Proverbs 16:9 NIV)

> "May he give you the desire of your heart and make all your plans succeed." (Psalms 20:4 NIV)

The Lord will give you the desires of your heart if you follow His plan and walk out the steps that He has for you. I believe this, and I have seen it happen countless times. I wish I had learned this way earlier in life, but I know it now. The sooner you start with this simple step, the sooner you will see the Lord move on your behalf.

> **"Write it out in big block letters so that it can be read on the run. This vision-message is a witness pointing to what's coming. It aches for the coming—it can hardly wait! And it doesn't lie. If it seems slow in coming, wait. It's on its way. It will come right on time."** (Habakkuk 2:2–3 MSG)

PRAYING AND PRAYING IN AGREEMENT

* * * * * * * *

You can and should be praying for your dream job. God will answer your prayer. Typically, He doesn't answer in the time frame we hope for, and He might give us an answer we don't really want. But we need to be asking Him and include Him in the process. If He is going to be your Ultimate Career Coach, then talk to Him, and talk often. Jesus said,

> *"But when you pray, go into your room, close the door and pray to your Father, who is unseen. Then your Father, who sees what is done in secret, will reward you."* (Matthew 6:6 NIV)

> *"Ask and it will be given to you; seek and you will find; knock and the door will be opened to you. For everyone who asks receives; the one who seeks finds; and to the one who knocks, the door will be opened. Which of you, if your son asks for bread, will give him a stone? Or if he asks for a fish, will give him a snake? If you, then, though you are evil, know how to give good gifts to your children, how much more will*

your Father in heaven give good gifts to those who ask him!" (Matthew 7:7–11 NIV)

"If you believe, you will receive whatever you ask for in prayer." (Matthew 21:22 NIV)

"And I will do whatever you ask in my name, so that the Father may be glorified in the Son. You may ask me for anything in my name, and I will do it." (John 14:13–14 NIV)

"If you remain in me and my words remain in you, ask whatever you wish, and it will be done for you." (John 15:7 NIV)

1 John 5:14–15 (NIV) says, "This is the confidence we have in approaching God: that if we ask anything according to his will, he hears us. And if we know that he hears us—whatever we ask—we know that we have what we asked of him."

Once you have written out your dream job or vision, it's time for you to start praying for it, but if you stop there, you have left off one of the most powerful tools available to you, the power of praying in agreement. Additional supernatural power is in asking others to come into agreement with you in your prayer request and asking them to pray with and for you. Jesus said, *"Again, truly I tell you that if two of you on earth agree about anything they ask for, it will be done for them by my Father in heaven. For where two or three gather in my name, there am I with them"* (Matthew 18:19–20 NIV).

I prefer team sports. I would rather watch a football or basketball game rather than tennis or golf. I like the team effort aspect, same with a solo or symphony musical performance. You could argue that both individual and group efforts are important and that one is not better than another; however, having everyone work together for a winning outcome gets my attention more. I believe that God probably sees it the same way. I am sure He likes seeing His children work together and helping each other out.

So what is the difference between a solo and a symphony?

- Solo: individual, usually knows the music and doesn't have it in front of them, one instrument only, a mistake is more noticeable, practice alone.
- Symphony: group, all have the music in front, need to play off the same sheet, a mistake by one doesn't get noticed as much, they are in agreement as to what to play, practice separate and together.

Which is better, and which sounds better? They are both great and both different. But why not make your dream job prayer request both a solo and a symphony? God's Word says for us to do both.

Now asking someone else to agree with you over your prayer request is difficult for most people to do. We don't want to ask others for help, and we don't want to admit we need help. But when we ask and include others, great things happen. The added benefits of having others pray on our behalf are:

- makes us get more realistic about our request (but you still need to think big)
- includes others in the process
- helps hold us accountable
- gives God more glory when the prayer is realized

I can ask you to pray that I will become the president of the United States. But will you in your heart agree with this request? Probably not. Remember what Jesus said about two or more agreeing. So my request needs to be a stretch, but it also needs to be something others can agree with. This needs to be our dream job prayer request. It needs to be big, but something that others would be willing to agree with.

Second, we weren't meant to be an island. We need others; others need us. I know I love seeing my grown children when they spend time together, help each other out, and genuinely want the best for each other. How much more does our heavenly Father want this for us? He wants us to work together so it's a win/win/win.

Win for the prayer requestor, the prayer, and God. He wants all of us to win when we work together. So don't be embarrassed. Include others in this journey.

Third, we need others to hold us accountable. When we invite others into our vision, we now have made our vision more of a reality. We are more likely to pray separately for our vision and take our next step. Most people who have started this process start working toward their dream or vision. It sounds foolish to write down your vision, ask others to pray on our behalf, and then just sit on the sofa waiting on God to act. So we are naturally more inclined to take our next step toward our dream because we don't want to let others and ourselves down.

Lastly, God gets the glory because everyone in the process knows that only God could have put all the pieces together for our dream to be fulfilled. In fact, most every time I have witnessed this in others' lives, God has opened doors and made jobs come into existence that makes us know that only God could have done this. A lot of times, the ultimate job is better than what we were even praying for. We end up praising God for making the impossible possible. So Jesus said, *"Again, truly I tell you that if two of you on earth agree about anything they ask for, it will be done for them by my Father in heaven. For where two or three gather in my name, there am I with them"* (Matthew 18:19–20 NIV).

If you are having a hard time asking others to pray in agreement for you, please go to our website, www.UltimateCareerCoach.com and let us know what your dream job is. We will pray for your dream job and you can also find others that you can pray for as well.

4

PRAYING AND
BLESSING OTHERS

* * * * * * * * *

To write down your vison for the future or your dream job and then do nothing else would be foolish. As a believer, you would want to pray about your vison to our heavenly Father. You would also want to enlist others to pray as well. But why stop there? You should be praying for others that their visions or dream jobs would come into being. In fact, if you can help anyone achieve their goals, you will be blessed.

In our small group setting, it is often someone who is seeking their dream job who helps a fellow seeker. Somebody knows somebody else who is doing what the person would like to be doing and can connect them together. So help where you can help, especially if you are in the same boat searching.

> "Do nothing out of selfish ambition or vain conceit. Rather, in humility value others above yourselves, not looking to your own interests but each of you to the interests of the others." (Philippians 2:3–4 NIV)

> "Carry each other's burdens, and in this way you will fulfill the law of Christ." (Galatians 6:2 NIV)

Now suppose you think you can't help others in their search. You can at least do the best thing, to pray for them. Pray that they would receive their dream job. Let go of your desires for a minute and put others in front of yourself. Do something different when you pray.

In this world, we normally put ourselves first when trying to win at life. It really goes against our nature to put others first. I don't know this, but I bet Nick Saban doesn't pray that the opposing team will have a good game and excel. I might be wrong, and I don't even know him, but I bet he doesn't pray for other teams to have great seasons, even those not in his conference. We are in a competitive world that doesn't seem fair. You think you need every advantage over others even when they are not even your competition. Somehow, we have come to believe that if someone else wins, we are the loser, that there is only a winner and a loser. That's absurd thinking.

God set up His creation to be a win/win/win. Jesus died on the cross for us to have a win/win/win. God wins, which He always will. We win, but so do others. Let's be in a posture of setting up a win/win/win. We do this by praying for others. And the Bible is full of verses about praying for others.

> I urge, then, first of all, that petitions, <u>prayers</u>, <u>intercession</u> and thanksgiving be made for all people ... This is good, and pleases God our Savior, who wants all people to be saved and to come to a knowledge of the truth. For there is one God and one mediator between God and mankind, the man Christ Jesus, who gave himself as a ransom for all people ... Therefore I want the men everywhere to <u>pray</u>, lifting up holy hands without anger or disputing. (1 Timothy 2:1–8 NIV)

> This is the confidence we have in approaching God: that if we ask anything according to his will, he hears us. And if we know that he hears us—whatever we ask—we know that we have what we asked of him. (1 John 5:14–15 NIV)

Jesus said, *"And I will do whatever you ask in my name, so that the Father may be glorified in the Son"* (John 14:13 NIV).

I suppose we all know that we should be praying for others: for it to go well with others, for them to get their dream job, and for them to see their vision for the future to come into being. However, we probably don't make time enough to pray at all, much less for others. I personally fall short in this area. However, when I make the time, I feel better about making the effort. In my earlier life, I wanted to succeed and for others fail so I would look even better. What a mess I was. What would this world look like if most everyone was succeeding in life and living life to the full? So why wouldn't we pray for others to be all that God made them to be? It would actually benefit our community and us.

> **"… if my people, who are called by my name, will humble themselves and pray and seek my face and turn from their wicked ways, then I will hear from heaven, and I will forgive their sin and will heal their land."** (2 Chronicles 7:14 NIV)

Maybe you still don't feel that motivated to pray for others. I get it. I think way too much about myself and what I want. I know I am too self-centered and need to change. One way to start that change is to pray for others even when I don't feel like it. Isn't that what real love is anyway? Doing something you know you should do even when you don't feel like it. I realize that when I follow through, even though I don't feel like it, my heart follows. If you lack compassion and empathy like me, pray for others. Your heart will start to heal, and you will find that you have become more compassionate and empathetic. So this exercise of praying for others changes your own heart. Jesus knew this, and that is why He encouraged us to pray for others and pray continually.

Jesus said, *"You have heard that it was said, 'Love your neighbor and hate your enemy.' But I tell you, love your enemies and pray for those who persecute you, that you may be children of your Father in heaven"* (Matthew 5:43–45 NIV).

"Therefore confess your sins to each other and <u>pray</u> for each other so that you may be healed. The <u>prayer</u> of a righteous person is powerful and effective" (James 5:16 NIV).

I know we should be thinking more about others and less about ourselves, but it's a win/win/win when we pray for them. We benefit as well. There are also several reasons for us to pray for others, which actually benefits us in return.

1. I want my faith to grow. When I see God answer my prayers for others, for some reason, they seem more impactful. I know I didn't do anything for this prayer to be answered and it was all God. As a result, my faith grows, and I assume we all want our mustard seed-sized faith to grow.
2. I realize that if God can do it for others, He can do it for me.
3. I feel more connected to those I am praying for. We all want to feel connected to others, and prayer helps. I am more likely to remember and ask others about something I am praying for that concerns them. I feel more invested in their life and want great things to happen for them.
4. I have gotten to the age where I want everyone to excel and be successful. I can't say this was always the case. But I know the world would be better if more people excelled in following God's plan for their life, and as the saying goes, "A rising tide lifts all boats."
5. When prayers are answered, God gets the glory. In theory, more people would turn to Him, and my world would become better.
6. I have become less judgmental and more sympathetic and empathetic, as discussed previously.
7. I realize how blessed I am. My problems seem small compared to others, and my God is big.
8. If I pray for others, others will pray for me. I have seen this every time we have a small group. People I barely know are praying for my success. Wow!
9. Then there are all of God's promises about blessing others.

> Give generously to them and do so without a grudging heart; then because of this the LORD your God will bless you in all your work and in everything you put your hand to. (Deuteronomy 15:10 NIV)

> After Job had prayed for his friends, the LORD restored his fortunes and gave him twice as much as he had before. (Job 42:10 NIV)

> A generous person will prosper; whoever refreshes others will be refreshed. (Proverbs 11:25 NIV)

> Serve wholeheartedly, as if you were serving the Lord, not people, because you know that the Lord will reward each one for whatever good they do … (Ephesians 6:7–8 NIV)

> Do not repay evil with evil or insult with insult. On the contrary, repay evil with blessing, because to this you were called so that you may inherit a blessing. (1 Peter 3:9 NIV)

Jesus said, *"Now that you know these things, you will be blessed if you do them"* (John 13:17 NIV) and *"Give, and it will be given to you. A good measure, pressed down, shaken together and running over, will be poured into your lap. For with the measure you use, it will be measured to you"* (Luke 6:38 NIV).

Paul said, "In everything I did, I showed you that by this kind of hard work we must help the weak, remembering the words the Lord Jesus himself said: 'It is more blessed to give than to receive'" (Acts 20:35 NIV).

Lastly, your heavenly Father knows what you need and the plans He has for you. Jesus said, *"your Father knows what you need before you ask him"* (Matthew 6:8 NIV).

> **"'For I know the plans I have for you,'** declares the Lord, **'plans to prosper you and not to harm you,**

plans to give you hope and a future. Then you will call on me and come and pray to me, and I will listen to you.'" (Jeremiah 29:10–12 NIV)

In conclusion, don't stop praying for your plans, but if you only have a little time to pray, pray for others first. I believe it will benefit you more than praying for yourself.

Again, if you are having a hard time asking others to pray in agreement for you, please go to our website, www. UltimateCareerCoach.com and let us know what your dream job is. We will pray for your dream job and you can also find others that you can pray for as well.

5

REMOVING THE STONE
OR NEXT STEPS

❖ ❖ ❖ ❖ ❖ ❖ ❖ ❖ ❖

What is standing in the way of your miracle? What is standing in the way of your prayer for the dream job, a better career, or a new business venture? We all have issues, and some are blocking the Lord from answering our prayers. What stone do you need to remove to see a miracle? When Jesus raised Lazarus from the dead, this miracle started a chain reaction that would lead to the greatest miracle of all, Jesus being crucified on the cross and paying the price for our sins and then being raised from the dead. However, before raising Lazarus, something had to happen so Jesus would perform this amazing miracle.

The Death of Lazarus
Now a man named Lazarus was sick. He was from Bethany, the village of Mary and her sister, Martha. (This Mary, whose brother Lazarus now lay sick, was the same one who poured perfume on the Lord and wiped his feet with her hair.) So the sisters sent word to Jesus, "Lord, the one you love is sick."

When he heard this, Jesus said, *"This sickness will not end in death. No, it is for God's glory so that*

God's Son may be glorified through it." Now Jesus loved Martha and her sister and Lazarus. So when he heard that Lazarus was sick, he stayed where he was two more days, and then he said to his disciples, *"Let us go back to Judea."*

"But, Rabbi," they said, "a short while ago, the Jews there tried to stone you, and yet you are going back?"

Jesus answered, *"Are there not twelve hours of daylight? Anyone who walks in the daytime will not stumble, for they see by this world's light. It is when a person walks at night that they stumble, for they have no light."* After he had said this, he went on to tell them, *"Our friend Lazarus has fallen asleep; but I am going there to wake him up."*

His disciples replied, "Lord, if he sleeps, he will get better." Jesus had been speaking of his death, but his disciples thought he meant natural sleep.

So then he told them plainly, *"Lazarus is dead, and for your sake I am glad I was not there, so that you may believe. But let us go to him."*
Then Thomas, also known as Didymus, said to the rest of the disciples, "Let us also go, that we may die with him."

Jesus Comforts the Sisters of Lazarus
On his arrival, Jesus found that Lazarus had already been in the tomb for four days. Now Bethany was less than two miles from Jerusalem, and many Jews had come to Martha and Mary to comfort them in the loss of their brother. When Martha heard that Jesus was coming, she went out to meet him, but Mary stayed at home.

"Lord," Martha said to Jesus, "if you had been here, my brother would not have died. But I know that even now God will give you whatever you ask."

Jesus said to her, *"Your brother will rise again."*

Martha answered, "I know he will rise again in the resurrection at the last day."

Jesus said to her, *"I am the resurrection and the life. The one who believes in me will live, even though they die; and whoever lives by believing in me will never die. Do you believe this?"*

"Yes, Lord," she replied, "I believe that you are the Messiah, the Son of God, who is to come into the world."

After she had said this, she went back and called her sister, Mary, aside. "The Teacher is here," she said, "and is asking for you." When Mary heard this, she got up quickly and went to him. Now Jesus had not yet entered the village but was still at the place where Martha had met him. When the Jews who had been with Mary in the house, comforting her, noticed how quickly she got up and went out, they followed her, supposing she was going to the tomb to mourn there.

When Mary reached the place where Jesus was and saw him, she fell at his feet and said, "Lord, if you had been here, my brother would not have died."

When Jesus saw her weeping and the Jews who had come along with her also weeping, he was deeply moved in spirit and troubled. *"Where have you laid him?"* he asked.

"Come and see, Lord," they replied.

Jesus wept.

Then the Jews said, "See how he loved him!" But some of them said, "Could not he who opened the eyes of the blind man have kept this man from dying?"

Jesus Raises Lazarus from the Dead

Jesus, once more deeply moved, came to the tomb. It was a cave with a stone laid across the entrance. *"Take away the stone,"* he said.

"But, Lord," said Martha, the sister of the dead man, "by this time there is a bad odor, for he has been there four days."

Then Jesus said, *"Did I not tell you that if you believe, you will see the glory of God?"*

So they took away the stone. Then Jesus looked up and said, *"Father, I thank you that you have heard me. I knew that you always hear me, but I said this for the benefit of the people standing here, that they may believe that you sent me."*

When he had said this, Jesus called in a loud voice, *"Lazarus, come out!"* The dead man came out, his hands and feet wrapped with strips of linen, and a cloth around his face.

Jesus said to them, *"Take off the grave clothes and let him go"* (John 11:1–44 NIV).

Jesus wasn't going to perform the miracle until the stone was removed. Martha didn't want to remove the stone, but did so after Jesus responded, *"Did I not tell you that if you believe, you will see the glory of God?"* Something had to happen before they could witness the miracle. Martha and the others had to perform an act of faith by removing the stone. The glory of God was waiting for them once the stone was removed.

Think about this for a moment and let this sink in… *"Did I not tell you that if you believe, you will see the glory of God?"* Do you believe? Do you believe that God wants to perform a miracle? The miracle is on the other side of the stone. Until the stone is removed, God is just waiting. And believe me, His patience is far greater than ours. *"Take away the stone."*

The stone could be different for each one of us. It is our next step. But if we write out our vision, have others pray in agreement for our vision, pray for others' visions to be manifested, and then remove our stone, Jesus will say, *"Take off the grave clothes and let him go."* I believe this with all my heart. I have seen it happen so many times in mine and others' lives.

Do you ever wonder what kind of witness Lazarus was after this experience? Do you ever wonder what his attitude and perspective were afterward? I believe that he touched many lives after this miracle. I believe the grave clothes were removed and he was let go. He was a new man, a man on a mission, a man with a new vison and destiny. I believe the same happened to Martha and Mary.

Jesus and our heavenly Father want this for you. They both want you to *"take off the grave clothes."* They both want to see you excel and be your best. Our Father wants you to be used for what you were created for. I believe they both would say, "You have been in the grave far too long. Now that the stone is removed, you can come out. You can now start to fulfill your destiny and make an eternal difference."

What is the stone for you? It could be unforgiveness, an addiction, an unhealthy relationship, laziness, fear, negative thinking, procrastination, debt, health, and so forth. What is it? You probably know without a whole lot of searching. Removing the stone could be more important than the miracle waiting to happen. However, some stones seem to be the size of mountains and don't want to budge.

Again, God's Word has an answer for this problem.

> Jesus replied, *"Truly I tell you, if you have faith and do not doubt, not only can you do what was done to the fig tree, but also you can say to this mountain* [whatever stone is blocking the miracle], *'Go, throw yourself into the sea,' and it will be done. If you believe, you will receive whatever you ask for in prayer."* (Matthew 21:21–22 NIV)

> Is anyone among you in trouble? Let them pray. Is anyone happy? Let them sing songs of praise. Is anyone among you sick? Let them call the church elders to pray over them and anoint them with oil in the name of the Lord. And the prayer offered in faith will make the sick person well; the Lord

will raise them up. If they have sinned, they will be forgiven. Therefore confess your sins to each other and <u>pray</u> for each other so that you may be healed. The <u>prayer</u> of a righteous person is powerful and effective (James 5:13–16 NIV).

Both verses say we need to pray. We need to seek our heavenly Father and our Ultimate Career Coach for help. We need to believe that He wants to help us and change us. He wants us to enlist others to pray for us as well. Everything starts with seeking the Lord and His kingdom. Jesus said, *"But seek first his kingdom and his righteousness, and all these things will be given to you as well"* (Matthew 6:33 NIV).

So here are the four steps in the secret sauce to getting the dream job:

1. Write down your vision.
2. Share your vision with others and enlist them to pray for you.
3. Pray for others for their visions to be manifested as well.
4. Remove the stone preventing the miracle.

In the preceding chapters, I have listed possible stones that might be blocking the miracle. Don't let the list overwhelm you. Look at the list of those that are past, present, and future and pick out the ones that resonate with you. I think all can be helpful, but start with the ones that jump up at you. This is not meant to be complicated. Faith is really not that complicated. We are supposed to take one step at a time. Pick one. Try it out. Take the next step and then pick another. The Lord will honor your efforts.

All pretty simple, right? I know it's not. The enemy wants us to doubt each step. But each step takes faith, faith that your heavenly Father wants something better for you, faith that He will help you to be all that He created you for. Remember, Jesus didn't come to earth and die on a cross so you would have a wasted or mediocre life. Jesus said, *"The thief comes only to steal and kill and destroy; I have come that they may have life, and have it to the full"* (John 10:10 NIV).

Isn't it about time to start living the life you were created for?

"It aches for the coming—it can hardly wait! And it doesn't lie. If it seems slow in coming, wait. It's on its way. It will come right on time" (Habakkuk 2:3 MSG).

6

LOOKING AT THE PAST

◈ ◈ ◈ ◈ ◈ ◈ ◈ ◈

Completing an Application (How Did I Get Here?)

I assume we all start out with big dreams for our lives, dreams of doing great things and/or making lots of money. I know I did. However, it doesn't take long for you to get beat up by the world. Before long, you feel trapped in a dead-end job and are just barely getting by. It looks like there is no light at the end of this tunnel and you will be stuck in this situation for the rest of your life. It seems that nobody cares about you accept your mama. And yet everyone else has the same struggle.

Our perspective gets jaded, and we become cynical. We start thinking, What does it matter? I will be stuck forever. It does not matter how much effort I expend; I will still be here a year from now. Ten years from now, I will die here. Satan wants us right there. He wants us to think these thoughts. He wants us to give up and quit. Most people I know stay in this rut and this perspective, never getting out, never reaching new heights.

So how did we get to this place? If you have ever filled out a job application, you know you wouldn't hire what you see on paper.

Filling out the application is like getting a root canal or paying taxes. The application sums up all you have done to date. It has places for you to give references from previous employers that can verify all you have claimed. Most people leave their previous employment with a bad taste in their mouth, their employers' mouths, or both. Most people don't want a future employer to verify information on the application.

If the employer doesn't verify the information on the application, chances are, the job is not the next best step. So you want a job where the new employer wants to know exactly what you have done and wants to believe what you have written.

This is scary. We need to take a good, truthful look at our past when filling out the application. We most likely don't like what we see. We are embarrassed. We start to ask ourselves: How could this be? What happened to me? What happened to all the dreams I had? Where did the time go? What is wrong with me?

Being honest with yourself and the application is tough. But you must start here. If you are going to continue to lie to yourself, another ten years will pass, and you will still be right where you are today. If you aren't depressed about now, you are probably still lying to yourself. I'm depressed just having these thoughts.

I imagine if we had to fill out an application for an interview to get into Heaven, lying on the application would only result in getting our application thrown in the fire. We wouldn't even get the interview. In fact, the application is what needs to be completed. God doesn't even want the resume. He doesn't even need to read past the first line of the application. And the first question and only question is: Do you believe that Jesus is My Son, that I sent Him to save you, and that Jesus was raised from the dead after He paid the price on your behalf? It requires only a yes or no answer. Then there is a reference after the one question, where Jesus will verify that He knew you and can vouch for you. Jesus answered, *"I am the way and the truth and the life. No one comes to the Father except through me"* (John 14:6 NIV).

I am so, so glad that this is all I must answer on the Heaven application. All I need to do is say yes and put down Jesus as my reference. There are no other requirements. Thank God! Thanks, Jesus! Now you can complete the rest of the Heaven application, but the only things that matter on the application are those things you did that helped others fill out the application successfully. Nobody in Heaven will care if you were a lawyer, a heart surgeon, or a bank president. In fact, those that will be celebrated will be those who made an eternal impact with their lives.

Imagine if Moses had filled out an earthly work application. He knew some important people growing up and yet made them mad. He doesn't appear to have had a real job for the first forty years of his life. Then he commits murder and goes into hiding for another forty years. All he has to show on paper is that his father-in-law employed him as a shepherd. Talk about gaps in employment. If you were a hiring manager, you wouldn't hire this eighty-year-old man to take out the trash. He even told God three times, "You have the wrong man for the job." I don't know anyone whose job application would look as bad as Moses's. If most of the men and women in the Bible had filled out an application today, they would probably have been depressed and discouraged.

Imagine if David had filled out an application as a young man. He was a shepherd for his father. As the youngest in the family, he wasn't even recognized as a leader by his older brothers or father. He claimed he had killed a bear and a lion, but there didn't seem to be any evidence that others believed him. (His brothers still thought of him as a baby.) Until he faced Goliath, who probably had a great resume, David's accomplishments were negligible.

But God can do immeasurably more with a person who is honest and ready to listen to Him. But guess what? The past is the past. We can't do anything about the past. But what we can do today, right now, can change the trajectory of our lives!

"Forget the former things; do not dwell on the past. See, I [God] am doing a new thing! Now it springs up; do you not perceive it? I am making a way in the wilderness and streams in the wasteland" (Isaiah 43:18–20 NIV)

So fill out the application. Fill it out honestly as if your life depends on it. Try to fill out every blank. Leave blanks if you must, but start by making this the best-filled-out application you can. Right now, only you need to look at it. God is **"doing a new thing"** in you and is **"making a way in the wilderness and … wasteland."** Now this gets me excited for the next step. If God can take Moses and do the miraculous, which He did, God can take you, and He "is able to do immeasurably more than all we ask or imagine, according to his power that is at work within us …"

Once you have a complete standard job application, you have done the hard part. Pray about it. Sleep on it. Ask someone to look it over and edit it. Correct it. Now copy this and use it as a master application. You can hand this out or use it to transcribe the information to any application an employer has.

Here are some links for a standard job application:

- https://dpuk71x9wlmkf.cloudfront.net/assets/2018/09/1018 2733/indeed-job-application-form.pdf
- https://eforms.com/images/2018/03/Simple-Job-Application.pdf

Almost all the applications have a pledge at the end that says that all you have written is true and correct and that you have not intentionally lied. Be honest. We can't expect the Lord to bless our search if we start out lying to get the job.

Now the Lord is doing a new thing in you and through you. He will make a way in the wilderness and wasteland. Just trust Him, but do your part. Be the best you can be where you are, and over time you can start to add and change your master application to improve it. You've got this! You can do this!

Accepting Responsibility (Ask Yourself: Have You Been Doing Your Best?)

Just trying to get by and not get fired is just where Satan wants you. If this is your attitude, what would Jesus say? He didn't die on the cross so you could just get by. He wants you to be bold, courageous, and effective. Again, Jesus said, *"The thief* [Satan*] comes only to steal and kill and destroy; I have come that they [you] may have life, and have it to the full"* (John 10:10 NIV).

To have a full abundant life, we need to start taking personal responsibility for how we got here and what we can do today. Let God handle the future. Let's focus on today.

Presently whether you have a job or not, you probably haven't been doing your best. Admit it to yourself and God. If you are bold enough, confess it to someone you can trust. "Therefore confess your sins to each other and pray for each other so that you may be healed. The prayer of a righteous person is powerful and effective" (James 5:16 NIV).

If you don't have a job, get a job, any job. I'm not kidding. Any job! There are jobs everywhere for those who want to work.

If you have a job, stop stealing from your employer. Now you might say, "I don't steal. I haven't stolen anything from my place of work, not even a paper clip." But if you come in late, leave early, take more than your allotted time on lunch break, play on your cell phone during work, cruise the internet checking out sports or fashion, or succumb to countless other meaningless distractions, you are stealing time from your employer. Just do your best. "Did you use to make ends meet by stealing? Well, no more! Get an honest job so that you can help others who can't work" (Ephesians 4:28 MSG).

Most unemployed people don't want a job flipping burgers because they think it is beneath them. However, all businesses are begging for employees who will show up on time, show up when they are scheduled to work, do what they are told, have a great attitude, and don't cause drama. I will go so far as to say that if someone would do their best and be exemplary, they would be promoted quickly. Businesses are screaming for honest, responsible people to take responsibility and do their best:

> Don't be misled: No one makes a fool of God. What a person plants, he will harvest. The person who plants selfishness, ignoring the needs of others— ignoring God!—harvests a crop of weeds. All he'll

have to show for his life is weeds! But the one who plants in response to God, letting God's Spirit do the growth work in him, harvests a crop of real life, eternal life.

So let's not allow ourselves to get fatigued doing good. At the right time we will harvest a good crop if we don't give up or quit. Right now, therefore, every time we get the chance, let us work for the benefit of all, starting with the people closest to us in the community of faith. (Galatians 6:7–10 MSG)

I own my own business, and I have not even done my best. I know it is hard, almost impossible. I get fatigued. I have wanted to give up almost every day. I have been planting selfishness and ignoring others' needs. I have been stealing from myself and God. I should have let the Holy Spirit shine not only on Sundays but from eight to five Monday through Friday, not to mention when I get home. I should have been working for "the benefit of all, starting with the people closest to ..." me.

What if we changed our mindset and said, "God is my employer, and Jesus is my immediate supervisor"? They both see all I do while I am working. Would I last in the position I am in? Would I get fired based on my past and present performance? I can be replaced. Everyone is replaceable. A lot of us look forward to replacing a president every four years. So everyone is replaceable. God can replace you in a heartbeat. However, He wants the best for you and me. He wants us to mature, take responsibility, and do our best. He wants us to represent Him in all we do.

So you have made some mistakes in the past. We all have. God has forgiven you. It is time to forgive yourself. Let the past go. There is nothing you can change about your past. All you can affect is this moment, which will start deciding your future.

"... for all have sinned and fall short of the glory of God." (Romans 3:23 NIV)

"Indeed, there is no one on earth who is righteous, no one who does what is right and never sins." (Ecclesiastes 7:20 NIV)

I once heard a preacher say to truly forgive someone else is to give up your right to ever bring up the trespass again. We all have committed trespasses that have prevented us from being all God intended. But what if you gave up your right to ever talk about how your past holds you back?

How often do you think or say "If only ... If only I had been born into a better family ... If only I had been born a different race, gender, or nationality ... If only I could have gone to college ... If only I had gotten the promotion ... If only I had married someone different ... If only I had won the lottery ..."

Stop with the "if only ..." Satan wants you to dwell on this. I have a bunch of "if only" statements, and when I start to think this way, all it does is make me bitter and resentful. Some of the "if only" are about others, and a lot are about what I did in the past. So stop using the "if only" about the past. If you want to use "if only," use it for the future.

"If only I could apply myself better at work today, I could get the promotion ... If only I could be a better spouse and/or parent, my family would be better for it ... If only I spent more time with God so He would direct my path, I would not stumble."

From this point forward, accept personal responsibility for past mistakes, stop dwelling on them, and start focusing on today.

Not that I have already obtained all this, or have already arrived at my goal, but I press on to take hold of that for which Christ Jesus took hold of me. Brothers and sisters, I do not consider myself yet to have taken hold of it. But one thing I do: Forgetting what is behind and straining toward what is ahead, I press on toward the goal to win the prize for which God has called me heavenward in Christ Jesus. (Philippians 3:12–14 NIV)

Jesus replied, *"No one who puts a hand to the plow and looks back is fit for service in the kingdom of God"* (Luke 9:62 NIV).

Letting go of the past will not be easy. Paul said we need to "strain toward what is ahead," and Jesus said we needed to put our hands to the plow and not look back. Both require effort and work. Let's be the first to accept responsibility when we make a mess. Let us be the ones who are thankful for our past because it has gotten us to a point of moving forward in a positive direction. God has a plan for you. He had a plan for you before you were born. He has a plan for you to prosper. He has a plan for you to have an abundant life. He has a plan to spend eternity with you:

"'For I know the plans I have for you,' declares the Lord, **'plans to prosper you and not to harm you, plans to give you hope and a future'"** (Jeremiah 29:11 NIV).

Forgiving (Letting Go of the Past)

I have been co-leading a Church of the Highlands small group called Faith to Find a Job for eight years now, trying to help people find a job. During that time, we've had a lot of unemployed people attend our group. Most everyone who came had a story about their previous employer(s) that was negative. Most were mad and felt like they had been mistreated. In all these years, I don't remember anyone who lost a job saying it was their fault. It was always their employer or supervisor.

We are all like onions. It would take someone attending our group several weeks before they would peel back the layer and start to share what was going on in their lives. The more they peeled back the layers, the quicker they were able to move on and get to the root core of some of their problems.

In some cases, others would come to our group, and the first question we would ask is, "So how did you find out about our group?" As soon as they were given the opportunity to talk, they didn't take a breath for the next twenty minutes, telling us how they had been mistreated by someone at their previous employment.

They went on and on. They were oozing unforgiveness. In some cases, I felt sorry for those at the workplace who had to listen to their complaints. These individuals were not ready to forgive those they perceived who had wronged them. And as long as I can remember, they never got a job until they forgave the other party.

Each time they went to interview for a new job, they were asked why they were terminated from their previous employment. I could only imagine they went off on how it wasn't their fault and the employer/supervisor was _____ (you fill in the blank). I was sure the person doing the interview probably said they couldn't hire the applicant because of the toxic attitude the individual still possessed. It just oozed out of the interviewee. They couldn't help themselves. They couldn't let it go and move on.

Only when they had had enough rejection and time had passed did these individuals start to see how toxic their unforgiveness was. As my pastor would say, "Unforgiveness is like drinking poison and expecting the other person to die."

However, I have seen individuals reach a point where they finally forgave their previous employer/supervisor. It was like a cloud lifted off them. In one case, an individual got a great job offer the next day after being unemployed for nine months.

If you were the one interviewing another for a job, would you want to work with someone who couldn't say anything nice about their previous employer(s)? Would you want to work along someone who had resentment, bitterness, and unforgiveness?

> Get rid of all bitterness, rage and anger, brawling and slander, along with every form of malice. Be kind and compassionate to one another, forgiving each other, just as in Christ God forgave you. (Ephesians 4:31–31 NIV)

I have always been told it takes two to fight or have a disagreement. I am assuming that a terminated employee may have been wronged to some degree; however, I am positive it wasn't 100 percent the employer/supervisor's fault. The sooner someone recognizes their part in the problem, the sooner healing can occur. Accepting our part in the problem and letting the other person go allows us to be healed and move on to bigger and better opportunities.

Jesus obviously thought forgiveness was a really big deal. So it must be. When He teaches His disciples how to pray, this is one of the items we need to pray about. Jesus said,

> *"This, then, is how you should pray: 'Our Father in heaven, hallowed be your name, your kingdom come, your will be done, on earth as it is in heaven. Give us today our daily bread. And forgive us our debts, as we also have forgiven our debtors. And lead us not into temptation, but deliver us from the evil one.' For if you forgive other people when they sin against you, your heavenly Father will also forgive you. But if you do not forgive others their sins, your Father will not forgive your sins."* (Matthew 6:9–15 NIV)

Of all the things in the Lord's Prayer, Jesus expounds only on forgiving others. Why would that be? It is and must be a really big deal. Forgiving others doesn't heal them; nor does it change them. Forgiving heals us and changes us. Isn't that what we all really need?

Jesus taught about being unforgiving in the parable of the unmerciful servant.

> Then Peter came to Jesus and asked, "Lord, how many times shall I forgive my brother or sister who sins against me? Up to seven times?"
>
> Jesus answered, *"I tell you, not seven times, but seventy-seven times. Therefore, the kingdom of heaven is like a king who wanted to settle accounts with his servants. As he began the settlement, a man who owed him ten thousand bags of gold was brought to him. Since he was not able to pay, the master ordered that*

he and his wife and his children and all that he had be sold to repay the debt. At this the servant fell on his knees before him. 'Be patient with me,' he begged, 'and I will pay back everything.' The servant's master took pity on him, canceled the debt and let him go. But when that servant went out, he found one of his fellow servants who owed him a hundred silver coins. He grabbed him and began to choke him. 'Pay back what you owe me!' he demanded. His fellow servant fell to his knees and begged him, 'Be patient with me, and I will pay it back.'

"But he refused. Instead, he went off and had the man thrown into prison until he could pay the debt. When the other servants saw what had happened, they were outraged and went and told their master everything that had happened.

"Then the master called the servant in. 'You wicked servant,' he said, 'I canceled all that debt of yours because you begged me to. Shouldn't you have had mercy on your fellow servant just as I had on you?' In anger his master handed him over to the jailers to be tortured, until he should pay back all he owed. This is how my heavenly Father will treat each of you unless you forgive your brother or sister from your heart." (Matthew 18:21–33 NIV)

Until you can let go of the past, you will never be truly healed. How do you even list the previous employer on a job application, knowing the new potential employer will call and inquire about you. I think this is why most people have a problem filling out a job application. The real thought that someone could call and talk to your previous employer scares the spit out of us. We know deep down that we weren't our best and deserve some, if not all, of what transpired.

So how many times should we forgive those who have wronged us? Do you really want to be the unmerciful guy? Let it go. Let God deal with those who have wronged us. Better yet, ask for forgiveness because of the trespasses we committed. Admit that we have wronged our previous employer/supervisor by the way we acted and preformed our job. The benefits of doing this are priceless.

> *"Have faith in God,"* Jesus answered. *"Truly I tell you, if anyone says to this mountain, 'Go, throw yourself into the sea,' and does not doubt in their heart but believes that what they say will happen, it will be done for them. Therefore I tell you, whatever you ask for in prayer, believe that you have received it, and it will be yours. And when you stand praying, if you hold anything against anyone, <u>forgive them</u>, so that your Father in heaven may forgive you your sins."*
> (Mark 11:22–25 NIV)

Don't you want your prayers to be answered? In fact, being unemployed or looking for a better job is the time we are typically most in prayer. And yet we wonder if the Lord is really listening to our problems. He is. We just aren't listening to everything He has been telling us about unforgiveness. Let it go. Believe me you will be thanking Him if you do.

One last thing, forgive yourself. Let go of your sins and past. God has. The past is the past. Let's make a point of moving in a positive direction from this point on. When we have made a mess of things, we need to accept responsibility for our mistakes and then stop doing the same thing over and over, just like the woman caught making a mess of her life.

> But Jesus went to the Mount of Olives. At dawn he appeared again in the temple courts, where all the people gathered around him, and he sat down to teach them. The teachers of the law and the Pharisees brought in a woman caught in adultery.

They made her stand before the group and said to Jesus, "Teacher, this woman was caught in the act of adultery. In the Law Moses commanded us to stone such women. Now what do you say?" They were using this question as a trap, in order to have a basis for accusing him.

But Jesus bent down and started to write on the ground with his finger. When they kept on questioning him, he straightened up and said to them, *"Let any one of you who is without sin be the first to throw a stone at her."* Again he stooped down and wrote on the ground.

At this, those who heard began to go away one at a time, the older ones first, until only Jesus was left, with the woman still standing there. Jesus straightened up and asked her, *"Woman, where are they? Has no one condemned you?"*

"No one, sir," she said.

"Then neither do I condemn you," Jesus declared. *"Go now and leave your life of sin."* (John 8:1–11 NIV)

We have all heard about this woman. We have all cringed at the thought that our sins could be exposed to others when we are caught. However, Jesus forgave her. He wanted her to move on in life and have a better life. I am sure she still had multiple problems when she went home that afternoon. I'm sure that life wasn't any easier; in fact, it was probably harder. However, I believe this encounter changed her and her life was never the same. I believe that later in life, she would look back and say this was the best thing that could have happened to her. Could you even imagine her being in a position to say she was thankful for that day when she was caught, accused, shamed, and almost stoned to death? I believe that on that day, her life changed for eternity.

Jesus wants to forgive us; we just need to ask. However, if you continue to knowingly sin, you are right back in the same ditch. Ask Jesus for help and strength to break the cycle of sin that has a hold on you. If you are reading this book, I know you want an abundant life. But you can't have this life if you are continually stuck. So forgive others who have wronged you. Forgive yourself and move on. Stop the sins that are destroying you and holding you back.

As a side note, I have been self-employed for thirty-five years. In that time, I have hired and fired many, many people. I am not the best employer/manger, and I am sure that had I done a better job of training and setting expectations on the front end, I would have fired fewer employees. However, I don't recall ever having anyone really accept their part in being terminated.

This would be a radical thought. What if we wrote an actual handwritten letter to our previous supervisor asking for forgiveness for the part we played? I'm not trying to debate the outcome or blame someone or something else, but actually accepting responsibility for our part and saying we were sorry. I would bet that we would be relieved. I bet that if we saw the person ever again, we wouldn't be embarrassed to say hello. I bet we would keep our spit if our future employer ever called them as a reference.

Even if you were never terminated or let go, send a letter to your former employer just telling them thanks for training you and giving you an opportunity. What do you have to lose if you wrote such a letter or even multiple letters? Maybe a little pride. But the gains of this exercise far outweigh the losses. Be bold and courageous and take a step that most people will never do.

7

REVIEWING THE PRESENT

* * * * * * * * *

Being a Good Steward (Doing Your Best)

Forgetting the past, we can make today count for the good. Jesus wants us to have an abundant life. How we handle today establishes what our future looks like. Let's make the most of today. Don't we want everything we do to prosper? David wrote the first psalm in our Bible and did a fantastic job of describing what a wise person should do.

> Blessed is the one who does not walk in step with the wicked or stand in the way that sinners take or sit in the company of mockers, but whose delight is in the law of the Lord, and who meditates on his law day and night. That person is like a tree planted by streams of water, which yields its fruit in season and whose leaf does not wither—whatever they do prospers. Not so the wicked! They are like chaff that the wind blows away. Therefore the wicked will not stand in the judgment, nor sinners in the assembly of the righteous. For the Lord watches over the way of the righteous, but the way of the wicked leads to destruction. (Psalm 1 NIV)

Don't you want the Lord watching over you? Directing your path? Supplying all you need? It seems to be what I like to call a no-brainer. Of course you do! Spend time in God's Word day and night. Seek Him in all you do now that you know He is watching you and wants you to succeed. He loves you and wants the best for you. So you must do your part. Be the best you can be. Make a difference in all you do. Stand out and be exceptional. Go the extra mile. Do more than is required. Come in early. Leave later. Remember, God is your employer and Jesus is your immediate supervisor.

> Servants [We all are servants and serve someone or something], do what you're told by your earthly masters. And don't just do the minimum that will get you by. <u>Do your best</u>. Work from the heart for your real Master, for God, confident that you'll get paid in full when you come into your inheritance. Keep in mind always that the ultimate Master you're serving is Christ. The sullen servant who does shoddy work will be held responsible. Being a follower of Jesus doesn't cover up bad work. (Colossians 3:23–25 MSG)

> Whatever you do, work at it with all your heart, as working for the Lord, not for human masters, ... (Colossians 3:23 NIV)

Jesus said,

> *"Who here qualifies for the job of overseeing the kitchen? A person the Master can depend on to feed the workers on time each day. Someone the Master can drop in on unannounced and always find him doing his job. A God-blessed man or woman, I tell you. It won't be long before the Master will put this person in charge of the whole operation."* (Matthew 24:45–47 MSG)

The best explanation of doing your best is detailed in Jesus' parable about the two faithful servants. Jesus said,

> *"Again, it will be like a man going on a journey, who called his servants and entrusted his wealth to them. To one he gave five bags of gold, to another two bags, and to another one bag, each according to his ability. Then he went on his journey. The man who had received five bags of gold went at once and put his money to work and gained five bags more. So also, the one with two bags of gold gained two more. But the man who had received one bag went off, dug a hole in the ground and hid his master's money.*

> *"After a long time the master of those servants returned and settled accounts with them. The man who had received five bags of gold brought the other five. 'Master,' he said, 'you entrusted me with five bags of gold. See, I have gained five more.'*

> *"His master replied, 'Well done, good and faithful servant! You have been faithful with a few things; I will put you in charge of many things. Come and share your master's happiness!'*

> *"The man with two bags of gold also came. 'Master,' he said, 'you entrusted me with two bags of gold; see, I have gained two more.'*

> *"His master replied, 'Well done, good and faithful servant! You have been faithful with a few things; I will put you in charge of many things. Come and share your master's happiness!'*

> *"Then the man who had received one bag of gold came. 'Master,' he said, 'I knew that you are a hard man, harvesting where you have not sown and*

gathering where you have not scattered seed. So I was afraid and went out and hid your gold in the ground. See, here is what belongs to you.'

"His master replied, 'You wicked, lazy servant! So you knew that I harvest where I have not sown and gather where I have not scattered seed? Well then, you should have put my money on deposit with the bankers, so that when I returned I would have received it back with interest. 'So take the bag of gold from him and give it to the one who has ten bags. For whoever has will be given more, and they will have an abundance. Whoever does not have, even what they have will be taken from them. And throw that worthless servant outside, into the darkness, where there will be weeping and gnashing of teeth.'" (Matthew 25:14–30 NIV)

So how does this parable apply to getting a job or a dream job? Work hard while the master is away. Don't use excuses like you don't know what to do or are scared of your employer if you make a mistake.

The first two servants didn't need directions other than make money. They took the next step and got to work. They didn't seem to worry about when the master would return, for they were doing all they could with what they had while they could.

I imagine they were all in an agricultural setting. One bought seed and planted; another bought sheep and grazed them. They both got to work doing what they could. Their success was dependent on some things outside of their control (weather, wolves, etc.). However, that didn't slow them down. I imagine what they did required a lot of effort and was real work. They worked from sunup to sundown. However, when they went to sleep at night, they slept great, knowing they were productive and did their best.

However, the last servant did nothing. He slugged around all day whining and complaining about his boss. He watched the other servants working and probably criticized their efforts. When this servant went to bed at night, he lay awake, worried about what would happen when the boss did finally show up.

I always ask myself, "Who would I have wanted to be associated with, the first two servants or the last one?" The last one looked like he probably was having more fun and wasn't worried about the future, but we know eventually it will catch up with him. I imagine his family was not very proud of him, and he would also know this deep down. It was a lose/lose/lose for him. He lost out. His family lost out. His boss lost out. And lastly, his community lost out. What a waste.

The other two servants were promoted and became even more trusted employees. I imagine the boss wanting to hear all about the challenges, problems, and successes each of the two faced. He could relate to their situation. He wanted to be friends with them. The last servant got fired.

Now what if the first two had suffered a loss even though they had really tried? What if the one farming had lost the whole crop because of drought? What if the shepherd had lost his whole flock to some thieves? Would the master have been mad at them? I think not. He would be disappointed, just like his two servants would be. But at least the master knew the two servants would do all they could to make good things happen. He could trust them again with a new assignment. The master knew we all make mistakes, but at least the first two tried. The last didn't even try and then tried to blame his own failure on the master. (As a side note, had the first two made the gains off something unethical or illegal, the master would still not trust then or promote them. If the master did, then he is the wrong master to be employed by.)

So the bottom line is this: If you want a better job or a promotion, do all you can do and then some more. Take a chance and not only do your job, but do something else that you know needs to be done. Your employer will notice, or another employer will try to hire you away. Not to mention, in the meantime, you are happier and less worried about losing your job. Others and your family will recognize your efforts even if they don't say so. Your attitude will be better. Your day will go better. You will be rewarded for your effort. Be patient. You will be acknowledged for your outstanding effort.

To get a better job, do the best job you can where you are today. Work hard. Come in early and leave late. Take a chance and do things that need to be done without being told. Work as if the Lord is your employer and Jesus is your supervisor. They are always watching.

Better yet, put a smile on every day, even if you don't feel like it. Feelings will follow the action. Others will want to be around you. Don't let the negative person bring you down or stop you from doing what you know could be done. Be bold and courageous with a smile.

If you do these things, you don't even need to fill out a new job application. I promise you will get a better job. You will be promoted, or someone will want to hire you away. Trust the process. Trust Jesus. What He said two thousand years ago is still true today.

One last thing, if you realize you have more in common with the third servant than the first two, dig up the talents and put them to work. Had the third servant admitted he had made a mistake several weeks into his master's absence, dug up the gold, and got a late start, the outcome would have been entirely different. It is never too late to get started doing what you know you should be doing. I suspect that when the master came back and the third servant had said, "Master, I was scared and took the easy path. I buried your gold and did nothing. But after several weeks, I realized I had made a huge mistake. I dug up the gold and put it to work. I did all I could do with the time I had left. I am sorry for my earlier decisions. I intend to not let that ever happen again. Please forgive me." What do you think the outcome would have been?

I really believe that all of us are more like this third servant sometimes. We aren't perfect and hardworking from the beginning. We have all made mistakes and buried our talents at times, taking the path of least resistance. We have all grumbled, complained, and whined about the circumstances. We have all made excuses and put the blame on others instead of accepting responsibility for our own actions. We all fall short. Thank the Lord that Jesus paid the price for our mistakes. Thank the Lord that He gives us multiple do-overs. Thank You, Lord!

Here are some verses that echo this same idea of doing your best wherever you are and at whatever you are doing. Jesus said,

> *"You are the light of the world. A town built on a hill cannot be hidden. Neither do people light a lamp and put it under a bowl. Instead they put it on its stand, and it gives light to everyone in the house. In the same way, let your light shine before others, that they may see your good deeds and glorify your Father in heaven."* (Matthew 5:14–16 NIV)

> *"If you're honest in small things, you'll be honest in big things; If you're a crook in small things, you'll be a crook in big things. If you're not honest in small jobs, who will put you in charge of the store?"* (Luke 16:10–13 MSG).

Luke 12:46–48 (MSG) says,

> The Master said, *"Let me ask you: Who is the dependable manager, full of common sense, that the master puts in charge of his staff to feed them well and on time? He is a blessed man if when the master shows up he's doing his job. But if he says to himself, 'The master is certainly taking his time,' begins maltreating the servants and maids, throws parties for his friends, and gets drunk, the master will walk in when he least expects it, give him the thrashing of his life, and put him back in the kitchen peeling potatoes. The servant who knows what his master wants and ignores it, or insolently does whatever he pleases, will be thoroughly thrashed. But if he does a poor job through ignorance, he'll get off with a slap on the hand. Great gifts mean great responsibilities; greater gifts, greater responsibilities!"*

Also consider the following verses.

Do not conform to the pattern of this world, but be transformed by the renewing of your mind. Then you will be able to test and approve what God's will is—his good, pleasing and perfect will. (Romans 12:2 NIV).

So whether you eat or drink or whatever you do, do it all for the glory of God. Do not cause anyone to stumble, whether Jews, Greeks or the church of God—even as I try to please everyone in every way. For I am not seeking my own good but the good of many, so that they may be saved. (1 Corinthians 10:31–33 NIV)

"And, oh, yes, tell Archippus, 'Do your best in the job you received from the Master. Do your very best.'" (Colossians 4:17 MSG)

"Do your very best." Wherever you find yourself and whatever you do, do your very best. Make sure it glorifies your Father in Heaven. Make sure that how you handle yourself honors your immediate supervisor, Jesus.

Spiritual Assessment (What Are Your Gifts and Talents?)

Do you really believe the following verses?

"Before I [The Lord] formed you in the womb I knew you, before you were born I set you apart; I appointed you as a prophet to the nations." (Jeremiah 1:5 NIV)

For you (God) created my inmost being; you knit me together in my mother's womb. I praise you because I am fearfully and wonderfully made; your works are wonderful, I know that full well. (Psalm 139:13–14 NIV)

Do you believe this, that God created you, that you are one of a kind? If you said no or are unsure, how do you answer these questions:

> How did we get here?
> What does life mean?
> How do you define good and evil?
> What happens when you die?

If you can't answer these four questions, I believe you will never find your real purpose. What you do will all be in vain and will not matter for eternity. Until you can answer these questions, please don't read any more of this book. Spend your time finding the answers to these questions. Your time will be better spent, especially for eternity.

Assuming you believe God created you and you are one of a kind and wonderfully made, the next step is knowing that God created you for specific tasks and a purpose. Why else would He have created you unless He has something that only you are uniquely qualified to perform and accomplish? I can't think of anything I have intentionally created that didn't have a specific purpose.

Do you know what you were created for? If you aren't sure what you were created for, how would you find out? The first step is asking the Creator. And ask repeatedly. Ask, "What is my next step toward finding my purpose and being all You created me for?"

> **"For I know the plans I have for you,"** declares the Lord, **"plans to prosper you and not to harm you, plans to give you hope and a future. Then you will call on me and come and pray to me, and I will listen to you. You will seek me and find me when you seek me with all your heart. I will be found by you,"** declares the Lord, **"and will bring you back from captivity."** (Jeremiah 29:11–14 NIV)
>
> If any of you lacks wisdom, you should ask God, who gives generously to all without finding fault, and it will be given to you. (James 1:5 NIV)

Jesus said, *"But seek first his kingdom and his righteousness, and all these things will be given to you as well"* (Matthew 6:33 NIV).

On top of asking, you should be reading the Ultimate Career Coach's manual and playbook, the Bible. This is your road map on how to live a life of purpose and meaning. This manual will guide you and give you wisdom on what your next steps should be toward finding and getting the dream job. You were created for a task or job that you will excel in and find purpose and meaning.

As a homebuilder, I understand the importance of using the right tool for the right task. You can use a hammer to drive in a screw. You can try to beat in a nail with a screwdriver. But in both instances, it will take more effort, make a mess of things, and frustrate the operator. The results are discouraging and embarrassing. If, on the other hand, you use the appropriate tool for the particular job, the results look professional, you can be proud of the outcome, and the effort spent is a lot less.

We are just like this. If you are doing a job you were not created for, the job can get done. However, the process is usually ugly and painful. But if you could find what you were made to do, life could and would make a lot more sense. You would feel like you are really accomplishing something. You could be proud of the results. As you get better and better at this, new opportunities will open up to use your talents in a bigger setting.

So what do you like to do? What are you good at? It only makes sense that if you could marry up what you are good at with what you like to do at work, you would naturally put more effort into your work. Why wouldn't we work in a job that we know we are good at and like to do? Our days would go better. The results of our labor would stand out. The customer would benefit from a better experience. The supervisor would have less problems. The boss would have a better, more profitable company. Your light would shine through to your customers, coworkers, and company owners.

There are all kinds of spiritual assessments, career quizzes, and aptitude tests online that you can take to see what you would be suited for. Take some and see if common themes run in them that point you in a direction to pursue. Print them out and show someone you trust to confirm your findings. You could go as far as showing them to a prospective employer if they match what they are looking for.

As you age and the season of your life changes, your direction could change. You might be ready for a different career or impact path. This is not a one-and-done. We change over time. The Lord is changing us day by day, so it would only seem logical that we could be more impactful in a different opportunity. Always be ready for a new door to open.

You were uniquely created by God. You possess special talents and abilities that only you have. You were created for a specific job. When you find out what this job is, you start to feel like you are running on all cylinders.

> For we are God's handiwork, created in Christ Jesus to do good works, which God prepared in advance for us to do. (Ephesians 2:10 NIV)

> Do not be anxious about anything, but in every situation, by prayer and petition, with thanksgiving, present your requests to God. And the peace of God, which transcends all understanding, will guard your hearts and your minds in Christ Jesus. (Philippians 4:6–7 NIV)

> And we know that in all things God works for the good of those who love him, who have been called according to his purpose. (Romans 8:28 NIV)

Again, trust the process. Don't be anxious. I have seen it countless times over and over again. Seek God's kingdom. Ask Him. Read the Bible. Do it every day. The right door will open, and the opportunity will be there. God will open the perfect door where you can use your specific gifts and talents. You will realize, "This is what I was created to do."

Resume (Your Personal Elevator Pitch)

> Where are you today in your career?
> Where do you want to be in the future?
> What skills and abilities do you have to offer an employer?

This is where a resume can start to highlight you above other candidates. For my money, I would rather have a completed application. The application helps employers compare individuals easier. But to get to the resume, you must start with a completed job application. If you haven't done this yet, don't try to start creating a resume just yet. Start with a standard job application form first.

Think of a resume as just a more pleasing-looking job application. The real difference is the first section of the resume. This first section can be called your job objective, summary of qualifications for a particular job, or chance to give an elevator pitch as to why you are the right person for a particular job.

So what is your elevator pitch? What summarizes your qualifications in a paragraph? What would be your career objective? Can you put this into two or three sentences? As we discussed, write it out, put it on the refrigerator, pray about it daily, and enlist others to pray for your career objective.

I personally have seen God answer the prayers of those who pray for their dream job daily. Writing out your dream job or career objective puts things into focus. Most people don't do this, and even fewer really pray about what their dream job would look like. And then even fewer enlist others to pray. However, Jesus said, *"Again, truly I tell you that if two of you on earth agree about anything they ask for, it will be done for them by my Father in heaven"* (Matthew 18:19 NIV).

2 Corinthians 9:8 (NIV) reads, "And God is able to bless you abundantly, so that in all things at all times, having all that you need, you will abound in every good work."

Look around and do some research as to what jobs line up with your qualifications and career objective. You need to be bold though. Your objectives or goals need to be greater than your present qualifications. But you have time. Look for jobs that you might be qualified for, which are on the path to your objective. Don't forget, while doing this, be the best employee at your present place of employment. And if you don't have a job, get a job, any job.

Think big. We have a big God. But be somewhat realistic. Asking someone else to pray about your career objective typically makes us more realistic and less in fantasyland. I personally think I could be a decent president of the United States, but I would feel foolish asking someone to pray for me to achieve this. However, I would feel comfortable asking my wife to pray with me that I would like to be a company officer in a large homebuilding construction operation. Back to Matthew 18:19, the prayer needs to be something we two can agree on and something I would work tirelessly to obtain.

So before you finish the resume and type up the final career objective part:

- Think big.
- Pray over it.
- Enlist others to pray for your career objective.
- Examine yourself to determine your desires and the real effort you're willing to expend.
- Research jobs that line up somewhat with your skills and career objectives.

While researching these jobs that might make sense for you, look for jobs where you might not have all the prerequisites. This could help you shape your career objective. Don't limit yourself and your future. Your career objective or dream job can and probably will change over time. God is changing us daily, so why wouldn't our objectives change? But you need to take the next step and then another. No one gets anywhere standing still.

I have read that researchers have discovered that when women apply for jobs, they feel like they need to meet all or exceed the requirements. On the other hand, males apply for jobs where they only meet 60 percent of the requirements. This explains why women are much more likely to get a job they apply for, but men get paid more than women.

We men tend to "fake it 'til we make it." This dynamic explains a lot about the sexes and the difference in pay scales and positions.

While both genders browse jobs similarly, they apply to them differently. Research shows that in order to apply for a job, women feel they need to meet 100 percent of the criteria, while men usually apply after meeting about 60 percent. LinkedIn behavioral data backs this up. Women tend to screen themselves out of the conversation and apply to 20 percent fewer jobs than men do. Moreover, women are more hesitant to ask for a referral from somebody they know at the company.[1]

Now if you have finalized your career objective and filled out a standard job application, the resume should be easier to create. If you are having a mental block, hire any number of professional online resume writers to start the process. Sometimes the cheapest is the best to start with, but you get what you pay for. But assuming they give it back to you in a nice format, you can tweak the words and edit it to make it more like you.

Most people become overwhelmed with the resume process, and it stops them. It really is pretty simple when you come up with your career objective or elevator pitch. Have you ever thought of God's elevator pitch or career objective? David did, and he hired God to run his life.

> Praise the Lord, my soul;
> all my inmost being, praise his holy name.
> Praise the Lord, my soul,
> and forget not all his benefits—
> who forgives all your sins
> and heals all your diseases,
> who redeems your life from the pit
> and crowns you with love and compassion,
> who satisfies your desires with good things
> so that your youth is renewed like the eagle's.
> The Lord works righteousness

---

[1] https://business.linkedin.com/talent-solutions/blog/diversity/2019/how-women-find-jobs-gender-report#:~:text=Research%20shows%20that%20in%20order,20%25%20fewer%20jobs%20than%20men.

and justice for all the oppressed.
He made known his ways to Moses,
his deeds to the people of Israel:
The Lord is compassionate and gracious,
slow to anger, abounding in love.
He will not always accuse,
nor will he harbor his anger forever;
he does not treat us as our sins deserve
or repay us according to our iniquities.
For as high as the heavens are above the earth,
so great is his love for those who fear him;
as far as the east is from the west,
so far has he removed our transgressions from us.
As a father has compassion on his children,
so the Lord has compassion on those who fear him;
for he knows how we are formed,
he remembers that we are dust.
The life of mortals is like grass,
they flourish like a flower of the field;
the wind blows over it and it is gone,
and its place remembers it no more.
But from everlasting to everlasting
the Lord's love is with those who fear him,
and his righteousness with their children's children—
with those who keep his covenant
and remember to obey his precepts.
The Lord has established his throne in heaven,
and his kingdom rules over all.
Praise the Lord, you his angels,
you mighty ones who do his bidding,
who obey his word.
Praise the Lord, all his heavenly hosts,
you his servants who do his will.
Praise the Lord, all his works
everywhere in his dominion.
Praise the Lord, my soul. (Psalms 103 NIV)

This is more than an elevator pitch. In reality, how do you sum up the Lord in several sentences? It can't be done. You will leave out critical components of His character. However, David wrote what he had experienced and seen in his own life about the Lord. So trying to fit the Lord into an elevator pitch could possibly go like this:

- Is forgiving of all sin for those who earnestly ask
- Heals all diseases
- Redeems those who are in the pits
- Pours out unmeasurable love and compassion
- Will satisfy your desires with good things
- Renews you
- Offers righteousness and justice for the oppressed
- Is gracious
- Is patient
- Does not treat us as we deserve
- Forgets our sins
- Knows how vulnerable and short our lives are here on earth

His benefits benefit the one who will obey His covenants and precepts. He benefits those in the third generation. He is in Heaven and rules over everything, everything. He is willing to have sacrificed His Son Jesus so we could spend eternity with them. His love is immeasurable.

Instead of hiring the Lord, why not go to work underneath Him? He has a job description for you. His job description is uniquely crafted just for you. Where has being your own boss gotten you? Maybe it's time for a change.

References (Good Character)

How do you get someone else to be a reference or advocate for you to get a better job? Most people don't want to ask. Either they are embarrassed or know they haven't previously done their personal best. We don't want to lie, but resumes and applications are sometimes full of lies unfortunately. Most likely, the person reviewing your resume or application has their doubts before they even start. They need to verify that what you have said is true.

If you have to ask a personal reference or a previous employer to lie on your behalf, you have already lost out. You probably shouldn't be applying for the job.

So where do you start getting references that count and will make the difference? As the old saying goes, "Sometimes it's not what you know, but who you know." Getting the right reference sets you apart from most everyone else. So where do you start? You start with yourself.

Would you write a reference for yourself?

Do you believe you continually put forth the best effort on the present job?

Do you believe you will bring energy and a good work ethic to your present job and future job?

Are you going to make a positive difference?

If you can't say yes to these questions, you probably need to start doing what it takes so you can say yes. Don't look for excuses or try to justify yourself. Start making a difference where you are. Start putting forth the effort that you would be proud of. Bring positive energy to your present job, even when you don't feel like it. Have a good work ethic: do your job, show up on time, be responsible, be the last to leave, and leave the drama at home. Let your light shine and make a positive difference regardless of how small the task is. Your character counts. In fact, some would argue that it is all that matters. In fact, give me a person of character and willingness to learn. I would rather have that person than a well-educated, smooth-talking individual.

As a believer, we know or have been told we build perseverance and character through our obstacles and challenges. Our failures help us to learn and become better. Be proud of the obstacles you have overcome. Those obstacles have shaped the person you are now.

> Not only so, but we also glory in our sufferings, because we know that suffering produces perseverance; perseverance, character; and character, hope. And

hope does not put us to shame, because God's love has been poured out into our hearts through the Holy Spirit, who has been given to us. (Romans 5:3–5 NIV)

As the saying goes, "Quitters never win, and winners never quit." Keep going and persevere. All the great role models of the Bible had obstacles and challenges. Some tried to quit multiple times. But they ended up finishing, and we look back and admire them for their character and perseverance. You can do it also! On top of all that, you have your heavenly Father that wants you to succeed and the Holy Spirit living inside you giving you the strength, courage, and wisdom to take the next step.

Now we know that character is a loose term that can be defined many ways in the world today. However, I still believe that Paul best defined character two thousand years ago.

But the fruit of the Spirit [good character] is love, joy, peace, forbearance, kindness, goodness, faithfulness, gentleness and self-control. Against such things there is no law. Those who belong to Christ Jesus have crucified the flesh with its passions and desires. Since we live by the Spirit, let us keep in step with the Spirit. (Galatians 5:22–25 NIV)

Therefore, as God's chosen people, holy and dearly loved, clothe yourselves with compassion, kindness, humility, gentleness and patience. Bear with each other and forgive one another if any of you has a grievance against someone. Forgive as the Lord forgave you. And over all these virtues put on love, which binds them all together in perfect unity. Let the peace of Christ rule in your hearts, since as members of one body you were called to peace. And be thankful. (Colossians 3:12–15 NIV)

The quickest way to make your character stand out is to be

thankful: thankful you have a job, thankful you have the health to perform the job, and thankful you have an opportunity to prove your worth every day. Be thankful.

I am speaking to myself right now. I have everything a man could want, and yet I know I am not thankful sometimes. I want to complain and grumble. Stop! Get thankful! Even when you don't feel like it. Feelings will follow. Nobody wants to be around a complainer and a grumbler. Get thankful!

Back to the original question: How or who do you ask for a reference letter? Typically, it is not your present employer. The reference(s) needs to be someone who has known you and knows your character. A previous employer is, in my opinion, probably the best reference. Please avoid a family member or best friend. But to ask someone to take the time and write a letter on your behalf, they need to believe that what you want them to say is true. You need to have exhibited good character.

In high school, I was barely a C student. I wanted to go to my state's university, where the entry requirements were less stringent. Other classmates who wanted to go to more prestigious colleges needed a teacher to write a recommendation letter. Those individuals had proved themselves in the classroom by the grades they made and the effort they put forth. I, on the other hand, was glad I didn't need a reference because I knew my effort was pitiful. The goal I had set for myself was a lower bar than my classmates, and it showed. Had I even started my senior year trying to put forth the effort and do better, I could have been confident to ask for a reference.

Bottom line: The way we perform has a direct correlation with our goals and aspirations. Start today setting a goal. Then start working toward it. Work as if you were going to ask your coworker or supervisor for a reference six months from now. Volunteer at your church or local nonprofit and work as if you were working for a reference. I know this sounds self-serving, but it really is a win-win. By your actions, you win, and those you work with win.

Set a goal. Be your best. Do your best. Be a person of character and integrity. Put forth the effort even when you don't feel like it. God will honor your effort.

> Whoever walks in integrity walks securely, but whoever takes crooked paths will be found out. (Proverbs 10:9 NIV)

> Blessed are those whose ways are blameless, who walk according to the law of the LORD. (Psalm 119:1 NIV)

Start today if you haven't started already. Walk with integrity and walk according to the Lord's outline for your life; everything will ultimately make sense and fall into place. If you do these things, it will not be hard to find someone to write a fantastic and truthful character reference letter.

No More Excuses ("All You Need to Say Is Simply Yes or No")

Excuses don't work. In fact, they work against us. We know this, but we still do this to ourselves anyway.

> "People with integrity do what they say they are going to do. Others have excuses." (Laura Schlessinger)

> "It is better to offer no excuse than a bad one." (George Washington)

> "He that is good for making excuses is seldom good for anything else." (Benjamin Franklin)

> "Never make excuses. Your friends don't need them and your foes won't believe them." (John Wooden)

> "Ninety-nine percent of the failures come from people who have the habit of making excuses." (George Washington Carver)

"If you don't want to do something, one excuse is as good as another." (Yiddish proverb)

What is your excuse? Does anyone really care? What excuses do you think God finds acceptable? Is there one? Granted, there are times when really bad things happen to people that were caused by others or circumstances that make things difficult or impossible. When someone overcomes those difficulties, we want to celebrate their victory even more. I get it that some things and situations are beyond one's control or responsibility. However, everyday excuses should not come out of our mouths. Jesus said, *"All you need to say is simply 'Yes' or 'No'; anything beyond this comes from the evil one"* (Matthew 5:37 NIV).

Does anyone want to hear why you were late or didn't get the job done? At my age, I have heard a lot of excuses, and I have used a lot of them as well. What would be great is to hear someone say, "Sorry I'm late. I don't want that to ever happen again. I will make every effort to prevent this from happening in the future." If they owned up to the part they played in the problem, I would be much more sympathetic, and I am sure others would as well.

What is an excuse anyway? I personally think it is telling half of the truth. So if you are telling half the truth, the other half must be a lie. Think about it the next time you get ready to put forth an excuse.

Adam and Eve were the first in recorded history to use excuses. Look at where that got them.

And he said, **"Who told you that you were naked? Have you eaten from the tree that I commanded you not to eat from?"**

The man said, "The woman you put here with me— she gave me some fruit from the tree, and I ate it."

Then the Lord God said to the woman, **"What is this you have done?"**

The woman said, "The serpent deceived me, and I ate." (Genesis 3:11–13 NIV)

They both disobeyed God, tried to hide, lied, and then made excuses for their actions. Their excuses are the culmination of multiple bad decisions. What would have been the results if Adam had not made excuses, taken responsibility for his actions, and asked for forgiveness? We will never know, but the results could have been less drastic.

I know I am much more likely to forgive and be empathetic when someone really comes clean with the reasons around their actions. Again, the older I get, the less patience I have for those who make excuses.

When we pray, God doesn't want a bunch of excuses. He knows what we are up against. He wants us to come clean and recognize the part we played in the problem. When we do, He can work with us. When we blame others, I suspect He says we are not ready for our prayers to be answered. (As I write this, I am speaking to myself.)

So in all we do, let's stop with the excuses. Let's take responsibility for our part and move on. We will move forward a whole lot faster. Excuses make us back up. And I don't know about you, but I'm tired of backing up. I want to move forward faster and with more confidence and courage.

This principle applies as well to my relationship with my wife and family. She doesn't have a whole lot of patience for excuses from me and is quick to call me out. I hated this at first, but now I recognize that she is actually making me a better person. I think I use excuses as if I am trying to protect my ego or what I think her perception of me is. What she wants is for me to be real and transparent.

Where we work, our employers and coworkers want the same. They want us to be real and responsible. You can move forward faster if you don't let excuses back you up.

> Do not conform to the pattern of this world, but be transformed by the renewing of your mind. Then you will be able to test and approve what God's will is—his good, pleasing and perfect will. (Romans 12:2 NIV)

> For we are God's handiwork, created in Christ Jesus
> to do good works, which God prepared in advance
> for us to do. (Ephesians 2:10 NIV)

God has great plans for you, plans to move you faster and further with more confidence and courage. Don't let your excuses get in His way. Nobody wants to hear them anyway.

Manna Jobs (Best Way to Get a Dream Job Is to Have a Job)

The best way to get a better job is to have a job. Even if it is not even close to your dream job, get a job. It will be amazing what the Lord will do when you take the first step. We call this a manna job. It is not meant to be the end all be all. It's meant to get you down the road toward your dream job or career.

Remember the Jewish people were in the desert for forty years after escaping from Egypt. The Lord supplied manna for them to eat and get by. Now they had to get up and go gather the manna each day. And they could only gather enough for one day. They needed to trust the Lord that He would take care of all their needs one day at a time. It took effort on their part while they were in the desert. Now I know this sounds difficult, to wander along for an extended period of time, but the Israelites didn't wander the first one and a half to three years on their way to the Promised Land. During this time, the Lord was taking care of them and preparing them for their destiny.

When they reached the Promised Land, they sent spies to check it out. Remember, all but two of the spies said it was impossible to take what the Lord had promised. Because of this, the Lord made them wander for forty years until a new generation of leaders was raised up. But then,

> When you have eaten and are satisfied, praise the
> Lord your God for the good land he has given you.

Be careful that you do not forget the Lord your God, failing to observe his commands, his laws and his decrees that I am giving you this day. Otherwise, when you eat and are satisfied, when you build fine houses and settle down, and when your herds and flocks grow large and your silver and gold increase and all you have is multiplied, then your heart will become proud and you will forget the Lord your God, who brought you out of Egypt, out of the land of slavery. He led you through the vast and dreadful wilderness, that thirsty and waterless land, with its venomous snakes and scorpions. He brought you water out of hard rock. He gave you manna to eat in the wilderness, something your ancestors had never known, <u>to humble and test you so that in the end it might go well with you</u>. You may say to yourself, "My power and the strength of my hands have produced this wealth for me." <u>But remember the Lord your God, for it is he who gives you the ability to produce wealth, and so confirms his covenant, which he swore to your ancestors, as it is today.</u> (Deuteronomy 8:10–18 NIV)

The lesson we can learn from the Israelites is that the Lord will take care of all our needs. He is preparing you for the Promised Land. In the process, He is "humble(ing) you and test(ing) you so that in the end it might go well with you." You need to collect each day the manna, which could be in the form of a job that is not exactly what you want. It will be humbling, and it will test you, but in the end, it will strengthen you in your faith and strengthen your character.

It does take time to find the dream job. Studies show that on average, it takes up to eighteen months to get the new job. During this time, gather your manna daily, trusting the Lord with the process. When the door opens, again trust the Lord that He is guiding you into the Promised Land. The Lord knows what you need. "And my God will meet all your needs according to the riches of his glory in Christ Jesus" (Philippians 4:19 NIV).

So having a manna job tells any new employer that you are willing to work and work hard, even if you don't like what you are doing. It shows character and work ethic. It will impress anyone you tell. So be patient, take the manna job, make the best of it each day, and trust in the Lord. He has a plan for you, a plan for you to prosper and not to harm you.

As a side note, I have met many people who have worked for ten to twenty years and then become unemployed. For whatever reason, they will not file for unemployment compensation even though they are entitled to it. They feel like it is a handout. It's not. You have paid into the Unemployment Compensation Insurance Fund all these years you have been working. You are entitled to it. It would be like paying insurance on your house for many years and then having it burn down. Wouldn't you go and collect from the insurance company for your loss? To me, it's the same thing. Collect your unemployment compensation while you diligently look for a job. This could be your manna while you are moving toward the Promised Land.

Health (Your Body Is a Temple)

If one of the stones that needs to be rolled away is a drug addiction or drinking problem, you know you probably don't need to be told. You are on the road to a slow, miserable death unless something changes. Being unemployed or underemployed is a time when you would be most vulnerable to these attacks by Satan. You may feel alone, hopeless, and lost. Drugs and alcohol will not help this feeling; in fact, they just make it worse. Seek help. Tell someone. Have someone you trust pray for you.

> And the prayer offered in faith will make the sick person well; the Lord will raise them up. If they have sinned, they will be forgiven. Therefore confess your

sins to each other and pray for each other so that you
may be healed. The prayer of a righteous person is
powerful and effective. (James 5:15–16 NIV)

Now you might not have a major drug or alcohol problem, but
are you taking care of yourself? Are you eating right, getting the
appropriate amount of sleep, and exercising? We all know what we
should be doing to take care of ourselves. I feel like this chapter is
beating a dead horse that has been beaten so many times, but how
often do you see it being played out in real life?

You know that if you physically feel good, you are more likely to
do better, have a better attitude, and get more accomplished. Not to
mention that during this stage of life, looking for a job can be the
most stressful thing someone can go through short of the death of
a loved one. Exercise. Take a walk. Get off the sofa. Quit watching
Netflix late into the night. You know all this. This is nothing new.
You have heard it hundreds of times.

During this season of your life, go the extra mile. Start a new
regime of diet, exercise, and sleep. Take care of yourself. Let's do
what we know to do and what the Bible tells us to do:

> If anyone destroys God's temple, God will destroy
> that person; for God's temple is sacred, and you
> together are that temple. (1 Corinthians 3:17 NIV)

> Do you not know that your bodies are temples of the
> Holy Spirit, who is in you, whom you have received
> from God? You are not your own; you were bought
> at a price. Therefore honor God with your bodies. (1
> Corinthians 6:19–20 NIV)

> So whether you eat or drink or whatever you do, do
> it all for the glory of God. (1 Corinthians 10:31 NIV)

Stop being a slave to drugs, alcohol, food, or TV. Come out from
under this bondage.

> For you are a people holy to the LORD your God.
> The LORD your God has chosen you out of all the
> peoples on the face of the earth to be his people,
> his treasured possession ... But it was because the
> LORD loved you and kept the oath he swore to your
> ancestors that he brought you out with a mighty
> hand and redeemed you from the land of slavery ...
> (Deuteronomy 7:6–8 NIV)

You were and are chosen, loved, and redeemed. Remember this above all else.

GOALS FOR THE FUTURE

Training and Education (Learning, Growing, and Praying)

Based on what you have set as your goal, do you need more education and training? Chances are, if you have set a goal high enough, you will need both. So even if you are waiting for your dream job, why wait to be trained or to learn what would be beneficial?

You can take all kinds of online courses to better yourself. The person who gets home and turns on the TV for the rest of the evening will most likely be the person who stays in the same rut. By taking a course, you learn needed skills and information, but something greater happens. The person who takes this next step, even though nothing else is happening in their career, starts to feel like they are moving forward. They become more confident and more empowered with their own life. It also tells a future or present employer that you are willing to do more and be more. It tells them that you are willing and want to learn and that you want to grow.

The old saying, "If you aren't growing, you are dying," applies to this principle. When you stop learning, you stop moving forward. As I reflect, the most exciting times of my life have been when I was learning the most. When I became a new Christian, I couldn't get enough of God's Word. I was like a sponge; it was all so new and alive to me. The same happens with our careers. Some of the best days were when I took on a new position or responsibility. I wanted to know all there was to know to help me succeed. Why wait for a promotion or new job to start the learning process?

Taking basic courses really made a difference for me and stood out to my employer at the time. While working for a large commercial contractor right out of college, I was put in the lowest-paid position on the jobsite. The guys sweeping the floors got paid more than me and were probably more valuable to the completion of the project. I felt stagnant six months out of college with an engineering degree. I asked my employer if they had any training or education programs. Well, they didn't, but for a company with thousands of employees, the question made it to the president of the company. Word came back down, that if I paid for the education and made a B or better, they would reimburse me. So I jumped at the chance to take a night accounting class. (If you have never learned accounting, this should be a prerequisite for growing up.)

For the next three semesters, I took one class each time. It was a hassle to go home, take a shower, and then go to class or do some homework on my off time. It was the first time I could remember really paying attention. A's came easy because I wanted to learn, and I had made this choice. Even though I was stuck in what I thought was a pathetic job, I got noticed. Each semester, when I asked for reimbursement, the report card made it to the desk of the president. By the third semester, the president would ask my superiors about my career progress on the jobsite. I hadn't done anything to be recognized on the site, but my local boss started giving me more responsibility and authority. In two years, I was promoted above those who were my elder superiors for no other reason than I can think of other than I took some unrelated classes in accounting and finance. Those classes had no relevance to my current job, but the classes were important because I had set a goal of someday being a president of a construction company.

For no other reason, take a course and learn something you don't know but would like to. I am telling you that it will broaden your vision and territory. The Bible says so as well,

let the wise listen and add to their learning,
and let the discerning get guidance—
for understanding proverbs and parables,
the sayings and riddles of the wise.
The fear of the LORD is the beginning of knowledge,
but fools despise wisdom and instruction. (Proverbs
1:5–7 NIV)

Don't be a fool. Fools go home after work and play video games all night and then wonder why they are stuck in a dead-end job. Now I was able to take these classes as long as I wasn't married or had a family. But use your free time wisely. There needs to be a proper balance. Sometimes I got the balance out of whack, and I knew it. We all know when we are out of balance; we just don't want to admit it or change. Nobody really likes to change. This next step takes real effort and sacrifice. However, learning something new will pay off way after the class is over:

Blessed are those who find wisdom, those who gain understanding. (Proverbs 3:13 NIV)

Hold on to instruction, do not let it go; guard it well, for it is your life. (Proverbs 4:13 NIV)

Instruct the wise and they will be wiser still; teach the righteous and they will add to their learning. (Proverbs 9:9 NIV)

The heart of the discerning acquires knowledge, for the ears of the wise seek it out. (Proverbs 18:15 NIV)

What education or skills does the person with your dream job have that you don't? Find out if you don't know and then find out the course you can take that will be your next step. Today, I wish I had taken public speaking so I could have been a better communicator and leader. I regret not overcoming my fears of being in front of people. Obtaining this skill could have helped me in so many ways.

By the way, if you don't have children and are not working twelve-hour days six days a week, don't tell me you are too tired at the end of the day. You can do this. You can learn something new. You will feel better about yourself and be more confident. The investment in yourself will pay off.

Dream Job (Being Specific and Setting a Goal)

I can't stress this enough, so I am repeating what I mentioned at the beginning. You need to set some goals and write out what you would want for a dream job. Be specific as possible. Really write it out. Look at it daily. Pray it daily. Have others you trust pray it daily. (Again, asking someone else to pray for your dream job makes us be more realistic and less in fantasyland.) But write it out. Successful businesses have a mission and vision statement along with short- and long-term plans. Why don't we?

(As I write this, I am sixty-two years old and have not done this in many years. No matter your age, this principle still applies. I am stopping right here to redefine my dream job, mission, and vision statement, and short- and long-term plans.) So again, write it out.

> And then God answered: **"Write this. Write what you see. Write it out in big block letters so that it can be read on the run. This vision-message is a witness pointing to what's coming. It aches for the coming—it can hardly wait! And it doesn't lie. If it seems slow in coming, wait. It's on its way. It will come right on time."** (Habakkuk 2:2–3 MSG)

Don't get bogged down with what to write. Don't overthink this. Just write the first thing that comes to your mind. This doesn't have to be set in stone and be for the rest of your life. This can and will change as you grow and mature. It could change once a month. Pray about it to your Ultimate Career Coach. Share it with your spouse or parent. Get their input as well. You can always modify and refine it.

I have seen countless times the Lord answers the prayers of those who prayed for their dream job daily. Now, I will say they did all they could do personally and left the rest to the Lord. In fact, some of those who followed this prayer plan actually received jobs that were better than what they were praying for. If we commit our plans/goals to the Lord, He is faithful.

> Commit to the LORD whatever you do, and he will establish your plans. (Proverbs 16:3 NIV)

> May he give you the desire of your heart and make all your plans succeed. (Psalm 20:4 NIV)

> But as for you, be strong and do not give up, for your work will be rewarded. (2 Chronicles 15:7 NIV)

Jesus said, *"Ask and it will be given to you; seek and you will find; knock and the door will be opened to you. For everyone who asks receives; the one who seeks finds; and to the one who knocks, the door will be opened"* (Matthew 7:7–8 NIV).

Seek the Lord every morning in your own private quiet time. Pray for direction, guidance, and wisdom. Pray for your dream job. Now most people say they don't have time in the morning for quiet time. They are too busy and have too much to do. However, Jesus really had way more to do and a shorter time to accomplish it.

> Yet the news about him spread all the more, so that crowds of people came to hear him and to be healed of their sicknesses. But Jesus often withdrew to lonely places and prayed. (Luke 5:15–16 NIV)

> and Jesus healed many who had various diseases. He also drove out many demons, but he would not let the demons speak because they knew who he was. Very early in the morning, while it was still dark, Jesus got up, left the house and went off to a solitary place, where he prayed. (Mark 1:34–35 NIV)

Jesus knew He couldn't do anything without His Father. He needed strength, energy, direction, and wisdom. All these came from the Father. If Jesus needed all these attributes, how much more do we?

So for the fifth time, write it out and pray about it.

> And then God answered: **"Write this. Write what you see. Write it out in big block letters so that it can be read on the run. This vision-message is a witness pointing to what's coming. It aches for the coming—it can hardly wait! And it doesn't lie. If it seems slow in coming, wait. It's on its way. It will come right on time."** (Habakkuk 2:2–3 MSG)

Searching (Stepping Out Your Comfort Zone)

The easy way to search for a job is on the internet. But I have found that sometimes that is the least productive time spent. You are submitting a resume or application for a job you probably don't care that much about, along with hundreds of other individuals. In addition, you have done it so many times to no avail that you don't even modify your resume to fit the job description. The search starts to seem fruitless, and you send resumes to some black hole in the universe. Then the next progression is that you get disappointed and depressed. I have seen it too many times. I hear of people sitting down at the computer for hours, filling out countless online applications day in, day out, and nothing happens. Same results day in, day out, and yet we are hoping for a different result, the definition of insanity.

Your career can be like this. Why would you do the same things day in, day out and expect to excel and have new opportunities? I believe the Lord has called us to be persistent, but when you are beating your head against the wall, it is time to try something a little different.

First step, pray. So often I forget to do this. Pray that the Lord will guide your time and your effort. Second, narrow down your search on jobs that really make sense or even look for opportunities that aren't even posted online. Third, do something more than the rest of the world.

If you are applying for a job online, print out a hard copy of the application. See if you know anyone at that business and contact them about the job. Find out as much as you can know about the company and the people who work there. The ultimate goal is to personally put a printed-out copy of your application along with a cover letter in someone's hand who can either make a hiring decision or pass it along to the one who can. Again, as the old saying goes, "Sometimes it is not what you know, but who you know."

You don't have to be best friends; the person hiring just needs to see the effort you are taking that puts you above everyone else who is applying. Be bold and unstoppable; however, don't be a stalker. It will pay off. "For the Spirit God gave us does not make us timid, but gives us power, love and self-discipline" (2 Timothy 1:7 NIV).

Be bold. I have witnessed people filling out the application and sending it out online in outer space, but before doing so, they have printed it out to get a hard copy. Then take that copy to the place of employment and ask for the manager. Once found, they simply say, "I filled out your job application online, and I really would like to be considered for the job opening you have here. Here is my application I printed out, and I just wanted to make sure it got to the right person. Thanks for your time and consideration in the hiring process, and I hope you have a great day." That was all. Guess what? Their application went to the top of the stack. They proved they were willing to do more than anyone else so far for the job, which we hope will show the employer something more.

In addition, so many jobs are not listed online or posted anywhere. Every thriving business is looking for dedicated, loyal, trustworthy, hardworking individuals. The employer is trying to make do with the staff he has because he doesn't think he has time to hire someone new and it is a hassle. But most businesses I know are looking every day for the right hire, even if it isn't advertised. So I go back to the principles in the Bible about sowing seeds (resumes/applications).

> Remember this: Whoever sows sparingly will also reap sparingly, and whoever sows generously will also reap generously. (2 Corinthians 9:6 NIV)

> Sow your seed in the morning, and at evening let your hands not be idle, for you do not know which will succeed, whether this or that, or whether both will do equally well. (Ecclesiastes 11:6 NIV)

One day, I was out of the office and came back to find a resume and cover letter sitting on my desk. Well, I wasn't planning to hire anyone so I immediately threw it in the trash can. Thirty minutes later, I pulled it out of the trash. As I read it, I realized I could use someone with this person's skills and experience. She had just moved to town, newly married and in need of a job. She had previously worked for a large homebuilder, so she went to about ten builders in town and dropped off her resume.

I called her the next day, and we set up an appointment. I wouldn't call it an interview because I still wasn't planning on hiring anyone. However, the more we talked, the more I realized she could make a big difference in our organization. The long and short of it, I hired her to implement a new purchase order system I had wanted to do for years but never had the time or right people. It wasn't long before we had changed over, and our profit margins edged upward under the new system. I look back and thank the Lord for giving her the boldness to sow her resume unsolicited.

The boldest I have ever seen was a soft-spoken woman who had been out of the job market for eight years while taking care of her ailing mother. She was so shy, but she got bold. She found out where the local Chamber of Commerce meet-and-greets were held every month and started going to them. She went way out of her comfort zone to meet others, and it opened up her eyes to the possibilities out there. It wasn't long before she had new confidence and a new job.

Lastly, I believe in the power of small groups. Join one or two. Open up. Be transparent. Tell others your frustrations and desires. Enlist them to pray for you while you pray for them. I have so often seen two unemployed people help each other with job ideas. We were meant to be in relationships and help one another. So often, we keep all this bottled up inside because we think no one cares or can help. Be bold! "Therefore, since we have such a hope, we are very bold" (2 Corinthians 3:12 NIV).

Your Purpose (Purpose and Work Intersect)

God created us on purpose for a purpose! So many books talk about finding your purpose. But when you mix purpose and faith, we think we are supposed to be foreign missionaries or full-time church staff members. Somehow I thought I needed to quit my career and go into full-time ministry. I have always had this lingering doubt that God wanted me to work in a church instead of a business ever since I accepted Jesus. Or at least I always thought this until recently. Now I believe I am right where the Lord intended me to be. I don't have the temperament right now to be working for a church. However, the Lord has called me into full-time ministry. It just happens to be at my workplace.

We are all called to be in ministry right where we are. Now if you are reading this book, you should be hoping to be moved into a position of more responsibility and authority. With this comes a greater sphere of influence, thus, a greater ability to make an impact in a country that seems to be getting further and further away from Jesus.

So if you can find the sweet spot where you are enjoying what you do and you are good at it, naturally you should stand out as someone different than most. This should give you a better opportunity to be a witness for Jesus just by your actions and attitude. So everyone's purpose is as Jesus says, *"But seek first his kingdom and his righteousness, and all these things will be given to you as well"* (Matthew 6:33 NIV).

As you are seeking the Lord and trusting in Jesus, your next overall arching purpose is to help others seek as well.

> Then Jesus came to them and said, *"All authority in heaven and on earth has been given to me. Therefore go and make disciples of all nations, baptizing them in the name of the Father and of the Son and of the Holy Spirit, and teaching them to obey everything I have commanded you. And surely I am with you always, to the very end of the age."* (Matthew 28:18–20 NIV)

We were all created to have these two purposes. But we were all gifted with different talents and abilities to achieve these purposes. So your purpose has everything to do with you and how you respond to the Lord and Jesus. However, we were all created uniquely to be used in different ways and to work together to achieve the same end results.

The real question you need to ask yourself is not, "What is my purpose?" The question is, "How has God, my own Ultimate Career Coach, uniquely gifted me to achieve His purpose?" What is unique about you over anyone else so you can be used for His purpose? Until we start to understand this and achieve His purpose, all we do is in vain, not to mention that we will never achieve all that the Lord intended us to be used for.

I still come back to my earlier analogy. A hammer and a screwdriver are both tools used to attach two different items to each other using a fastener. However, using a hammer to drive in a screw can be done but leaves an undesired result. A nail can be driven in with a screwdriver with a whole lot of effort and results in an ugly mess. Both tools are for the same ultimate purpose but need to be used totally different, and when used right, the result is fast, efficient, and professional. How do you know what tool you were meant to be?

Jesus said,

> *"I am the vine; you are the branches. If you remain in me and I in you, you will bear much fruit; apart from me you can do nothing. If you do not remain in me, you are like a branch that is thrown away and withers; such branches are picked up, thrown into the fire and*

burned. If you remain in me and my words remain in you, ask whatever you wish, and it will be done for you. This is to my Father's glory, that you bear much fruit, showing yourselves to be my disciples." (John 15:5–8 NIV)

We were meant to be attached to Jesus. Separated from Him and not attached, we can do nothing of real positive eternal significance. You just need to figure out what tool you are. And this could change as you mature because the Lord is transforming you into a new creation. "Therefore, if anyone is in Christ, the new creation has come: The old has gone, the new is here!" (2 Corinthians 5:17 NIV).

Are you doing the very thing God called you to do? Are you allowing God to use you for His purpose? What talents and abilities do you possess that you could use to achieve His purpose? He designed you specifically to glorify Him and point others to Him. Ask yourself:

1. Natural Talents: What ability do you naturally possess?
2. Spiritual Gifts: What are your primary motivational gifts?
3. Inward Design: What do you really want to do?
4. Results and Fruit: Where does your life produce the most?
5. Affirmation and Recognition: What do others affirm about you?
6. Passion and Convictions: What are you compelled to pursue?
7. Circumstances and Opportunity: What opportunity is in front of you now?

When you can start to answer these questions, you will realize that the Lord created you for His purpose to perform a specific task that only you can be used for. He has a destiny for you to fulfill. Then you will be able to say, "I was made for this! I was made to be used like this."

Where we spend most of our waking productive hours at work, we are supposed to be fulfilling His purpose. Therefore, is everything you do at work honoring the Lord? By your efforts and attitude, would someone see you are different? You were called to stand out, to be holy. (The dictionary defines "holy" as "dedicated or consecrated to God or a religious purpose; sacred.") Are you dedicated to the Lord and His purpose?

> But just as he who called you is holy, so be holy in all you do; for it is written: **"Be holy, because I am holy."** (1 Peter 1:15–16 NIV)

When you figure out where you fit into the Lord's purpose and start to do the part you were created to do, only then will you find the true meaning of your life and feel on point. Do not let this overwhelm you. I am still trying to understand what tool I was created to be. But I know I get more and more lost the more I concentrate on finding out what my purpose is instead of seeking His purpose and getting on board with His plan.

All this to say is that our purpose should be His purpose. Our careers should be overlapped with His purpose. Our career is just a type of tool He is using to fulfill His purpose. He wants to attach two things together. He wants to attach us to Jesus, and He wants others to be attached to Jesus. When we and others are attached to Jesus, we are made holy in His sight. I think we all want to hear the Lord tell us what Jesus said. *"His master replied, 'Well done, good and faithful servant! You have been faithful with a few things; I will put you in charge of many things. Come and share your master's happiness!'"* (Matthew 25:21 NIV).

Have you ever realized that a servant probably doesn't wonder what his purpose in life is? He knows his purpose, to do his master's will. It's his master's purpose that matters, not his. The servant just does a great job at whatever he knows he needs to do to accomplish what his master wants. The servant seeks to accomplish his master's purpose. And in doing so, he is rewarded. These rewards don't have to be financial either. The biggest reward is not more responsibility but to share in the master's happiness.

Don't get bogged down on trying to figure out your purpose. (I have spent the last twenty years trying to figure this out and haven't.) Start seeking His purpose where you work. You are a tool he wants to use that, when used right, will be fast, efficient, and professional. You will be excited to see what the Lord does through you and in you as you play a part in His plan and purpose. He will take care of your next placement; you just need to be the best tool possible where you are. When you do this, you will be able to say, "I was made for this! I was made to be used like this."

Being a Blessing (Blessing and Praying for Others)

If you are reading this book, you want to excel and be different. You want to be a better leader, a better citizen, a better spouse, or a better parent, just a better you. One of the goals of reading your Bible should be for you to be a better you. You are called to be different. You are called to stand out. You are called to be a light and to shine. Jesus said,

> *"You* [put your name here] *are the light of the world. A town built on a hill cannot be hidden. Neither do people light a lamp and put it under a bowl. Instead they put it on its stand, and it gives light to everyone in the house. In the same way, let your light shine before others, that they may see your good deeds and glorify your Father in heaven."* (Matthew 5:14–16 NIV)

One of the best ways to let your light shine and be different is to be a blessing to others. Now, I have met plenty of people who were unemployed or thought they were stuck in a dead-end job. Their typical focus is on themselves and why they are stuck. They blame others or the system. Most of the words coming out of their mouth start with "I" and "me." Most did have legitimate problems and complaints, but that typically got them nowhere and kept them stuck.

> Do nothing out of selfish ambition or vain conceit. Rather, in humility value others above yourselves,

> not looking to your own interests but each of you to
> the interests of the others. (Philippians 2:3–4 NIV)

The best way to get unstuck in a dead-end job or if you are unemployed is to start being a blessing for others. You can do this, and it does not have to cost you a dime. It only costs you time and effort, which most people have when they find themselves floundering. Stop focusing on me and start helping others. Start by cleaning up where you live. You might like the trash and clutter because it goes along with your feelings right now, but nobody else likes it. Clean up some trash in the street, help the widow down the street who needs some repairs, listen to someone who is lonely, and so forth. Help where you see there is a need. Needs are everywhere.

You still need to do your part to find a better job or get a job, but you have time to still make a difference. Get off the sofa. Put a smile on your face, even if you don't feel like it. Go out the front door and see where you can help. Look. Help is needed everywhere. I know you need help. Your heavenly Father knows you need help, and He is trying to help you. You just keep getting in the way. Treat others the way you wish they would treat you. Jesus said, *"Do to others as you would have them do to you"* (Luke 6:31 NIV).

When we stop focusing on ourselves and start reaching out to others, our whole world starts to change. I can't explain how this happens, but it might as well be a natural law. However, it definitely is a spiritual law. Jesus said, *"Give, and it will be given to you. A good measure, pressed down, shaken together and running over, will be poured into your lap. For with the measure you use, it will be measured to you"* (Luke 6:38 NIV).

> A generous person will prosper; whoever refreshes
> others will be refreshed. (Proverbs 11:25 NIV)

> Whatever you do, work at it with all your heart, as
> working for the Lord, not for human masters, since
> you know that you will receive an inheritance from
> the Lord as a reward. It is the Lord Christ you are
> serving. (Colossians 3:23–24 NIV)

Now, the biggest help you can offer someone will cost you nothing but time. Pray. Pray for others. Your Father in Heaven knows what you need, so change the subject next time you meet with Him. Pray for others. If you want a better job, pray for others to get a better job. If you want a job, pray that others get a job. If you want better health, pray for others to have better health. In fact, this should be the first thing we do as Christians.

> I urge, then, first of all, that petitions, prayers, intercession and thanksgiving be made for all people— (1 Timothy 2:1 NIV)

> After Job had prayed for his friends, the LORD restored his fortunes and gave him twice as much as he had before. (Job 42:10 NIV)

Chances are, you have never suffered like Job. Better yet, Job would have said you are extremely blessed. But even in all Job's pain and suffering with no end in sight, he prayed for his friends. Not for himself, but for his friends. When he stopped focusing on himself and started focusing on others, his whole world changed. This can happen to you as well.

Then when you see the prayers answered, be positive, rejoice, and be thankful. Be thankful that your heavenly Father answered your prayers. "And whatever you do, whether in word or deed, do it all in the name of the Lord Jesus, giving thanks to God the Father through him" (Colossians 3:17 NIV).

Give thanks. Tell your heavenly Father thanks. Tell others that you are thankful for them. Thank people when they try to help you find a better job. Send a handwritten thank-you note to anyone you interview with or is helpful. Show some genuine gratitude. This is blessing people by making them feel like they were helpful. You want to be recognized and thanked, so do others. You will feel better about yourself when you start to look and express the good in others.

Pray for others. Be a blessing, and you will be blessed.

Be Strong and Courageous (Not Who You Are, But Whose You Are and Who Is With You)

When feeling like you are in a dead-end job or unemployed, you might feel that the Lord has forgotten about you. You might even feel that you will be stuck right where you are for the rest of your life.

If we could just grasp how much God loves us, if we could just grasp that He took time to create us for a reason, a unique reason, imagine Him saying, "I created you for such a day as this. You have certain characteristics and talents that only you possess. I have planned that you will do this certain task to change others' destinies that only you are qualified to do. And lastly, I love you so much because you are Mine. My mark is all over you. I want you to have a great life, and I want to spend time with you and all your siblings now and for eternity. I chose you to display My glory. However, everything hinges on who you say Jesus was, is, and will be."

So be bold! Be strong! Be courageous! Be daring! The Lord goes with you! Before Moses leaves the Israelites to die, he tells Joshua, "Be strong and courageous. Do not be afraid or terrified because of them, for the LORD your God goes with you; he will never leave you nor forsake you" (Deuteronomy 31:6 NIV).

After the death of Moses, the servant of the Lord, the Lord said to Joshua,

> **"Be strong and very courageous. Be careful to obey all the law my servant Moses gave you; do not turn from it to the right or to the left, that you may be successful wherever you go. Keep this Book of the Law always on your lips; meditate on it day and night, so that you may be careful to do everything written in it. Then you will be prosperous and successful. Have I not commanded you? Be strong and courageous. Do not be afraid; do not be discouraged, for the Lord your God will be with you wherever you go."** (Joshua 1:1, 7–9 NIV)

Why would the Lord need to command Joshua to be strong and courageous? Why would Moses need to tell Joshua to be strong and courageous? Joshua was the one with Caleb who came back and said that with the Lord, the Israelites could conquer the giants in the Promised Land. He had previously led the Israelites into battle and won. He had been successful and set apart. Now he is approaching eighty years old, but physically he still felt like a young man. He had been a slave for the first forty years of his life and then wandered in the desert for another forty years as an assistant for Moses. He has seen all his contemporaries die, and he and Caleb are the only men around eighty entering Israel with the next oldest being around sixty. He was much older and much more experienced than anyone else. He had been Moses' right-hand man. He was one of the few who remembered what it meant to be a slave and then cross the Red Sea. So why would the Lord need to command Joshua to be strong and courageous?

I believe that we are all weak and need encouragement. I have read that some of the best leaders need the most encouragement. They need to be told they can do it. You can do it! You need others to tell you that you can do it. You need to hear or feel the Lord telling you that you can do it too. The Lord tells Joshua to **"be strong and courageous"** and then commands him to **"be strong and courageous."** He is telling you the same thing.

On top of this, the Israelites, those he was leading, also had to tell Joshua to be strong and courageous.

> Then they answered Joshua, "Whatever you have commanded us we will do, and wherever you send us we will go. Just as we fully obeyed Moses, so we will obey you. Only may the LORD your God be with you as he was with Moses. Whoever rebels against your word and does not obey it, whatever you may command them, will be put to death. Only be strong and courageous!" (Joshua 1:16–18 NIV)

The Lord is telling us to **"be strong and courageous."** Why?

George Goodwyn Jr.

Because He has great things in store for you, but they will take effort. Nobody needs to be strong and courageous lying on the sofa with a remote control in their hand. We need to be strong and courageous when the world and everything we see seem to be stacked up against us. But what could stand in the way of you with the Lord by your side? He just asks you to take the first step in faith, knowing He will be with you every step of the way.

> "The Lord is with you when you are with him. If you seek him, he will be found by you, but if you forsake him, he will forsake you ..." But as for you, be strong and do not give up, for your work will be rewarded."
> (2 Chronicles 15:2,7 NIV)

Be confident that your faith and effort will be rewarded. The Lord will not forsake you. You were chosen for such a time as this.

> **"I took you from the ends of the earth, from its farthest corners I called you. I said, 'You are my servant'; I have chosen you and have not rejected you. So do not fear, for I am with you; do not be dismayed, for I am your God. I will strengthen you and help you; I will uphold you with my righteous right hand ... For I am the LORD your God who takes hold of your right hand and says to you, Do not fear; I will help you."** (Isaiah 41:9–10, 13 NIV)

> I remain confident of this: I will see the goodness of the Lord in the land of the living. Wait for the Lord; be strong and take heart and wait for the Lord. (Psalm 24:13–14 NIV)

> Love the Lord, all his faithful people! The Lord preserves those who are true to him, but the proud he pays back in full. Be strong and take heart, all you who hope in the Lord. (Psalm 31:23–24 NIV)

> Now faith [your next step] is confidence in what we hope for and assurance about what we do not see. (Hebrews 11:1 NIV)

> But you are a chosen people, a royal priesthood, a holy nation, God's special possession, that you may declare the praises of him who called you out of darkness into his wonderful light. Once you were not a people, but now you are the people of God; once you had not received mercy, but now you have received mercy. (1 Peter 2:9–10 NIV)

King David tells his son, Solomon, the following before he dies, "Then you will have success if you are careful to observe the decrees and laws that the LORD gave Moses for Israel. Be strong and courageous. Do not be afraid or discouraged" (1 Chronicles 22:13 NIV).

But Jesus immediately said to them, *"Take courage! It is I. Don't be afraid"* (Matthew 14:27 NIV).

Also consider the following verses:

> Be on your guard; stand firm in the faith; be courageous; be strong. (1 Corinthians 16:13 NIV)

> **"I will lead the blind by ways they have not known, along unfamiliar paths I will guide them; I will turn the darkness into light before them and make the rough places smooth. These are the things I will do; I will not forsake them."** (Isaiah 42:16 NIV)

> So we say with confidence, "The Lord is my helper; I will not be afraid. What can mere mortals do to me?" (Hebrews 13:6 NIV)

So be strong and courageous in your job search. The Lord will be with you if you seek Him first. He wants to be your Helper and for you not to be afraid. He will lead you if you let Him.

As a side note, I believe others want to follow and be associated with leaders committed to Jesus, obey God's Word, and are strong and courageous because the Lord is with them. Think about this: the alternative is a leader committed to themselves, does what they want to do regardless of whether it is right or wrong, and then does it all on their own strength. Would you want to follow or be associated with this type of leader? What type of leader do you want to be? You are a leader whether you realize it or not. So be strong and courageous for the right reasons, for eternal reasons.

Guidance and Wisdom (Networking)

Who likes to get directions or advice? I know I don't. I don't like to tell others I'm lost and confused. It makes me feel inferior. Also when you are young, you think you know everything, and only as you get older do you realize that you know less and less.

At sixty-two, I have finally gotten a personal coach, and it's the best thing that has happened to me in a while. He has challenged me and given me ideas for possible new directions. He wants me to succeed and make an eternal difference. He has also advised me to come up with a personal board of directors, which seems so foreign to me. It seems strange that I would have a few people I would discuss big decisions with that affect me, my family, and my sphere of influence.

Lastly, my coach wanted me to connect with another man going through a similar life series of events he knew. I didn't want to bother this stranger and felt intimidated. I felt like he had better things to do than waste his time on me. (That was foolish thinking.) I finally met with him after three different promptings from my coach and found out how wrong I was. He was a great help and blessing.

People genuinely want to help others. I know they seem busy, but they want to encourage someone else. They want to encourage you. They feel better about themselves when they help you. You will feel better about yourself when you help others. I think everyone wants a mentor and wants to be a mentor to someone else. So what's stopping us from letting our guard down and asking. You would be surprised at how fast others want to help if you are open and receptive to what they have to say.

When looking for a job or a better job, those that included others in the process were more likely to get the dream job faster. It helped to have others give them advice on things they might not have been aware of. So ask. You don't have anything to lose except maybe your pride. You have everything to gain. The wisest man to ever live, Solomon, was all about seeking advice, getting counsel, and seeking wisdom.

> let the wise listen and add to their learning, and let the discerning get guidance— (Proverbs 1:5 NIV)

> Without good direction, people lose their way; the more wise counsel you follow, the better your chances. (Proverbs 11:14 NIV)

> From the fruit of their lips people are filled with good things, and the work of their hands brings them reward. The way of fools seems right to them, but the wise listen to advice. (Proverbs 12:14–15 NIV)

> Where there is strife, there is pride, but wisdom is found in those who take advice. (Proverbs 13:10 NIV)

> Refuse good advice and watch your plans fail; take good counsel and watch them succeed. (Proverbs 15:22 MSG)

> Listen to advice and accept discipline, and at the end you will be counted among the wise. (Proverbs 19:20 NIV)

> As iron sharpens iron, so one person sharpens another. (Proverbs 27:17 NIV)

So where do you start looking for advice, counseling, wisdom, and networking? Why your local church, of course. Join a small group. Serve on a team. Let others know the real you and the things you struggle with and the things you hope for in the future. Others want to help. It really is that simple if you are willing to be transparent and humble. This goes against our very sinful nature. Try it though.

On top of that, find a mentor and be a mentor. Again, the best place to find a mentor is at your church. Look around. Plenty of men and women have gone down the same road you are on and have a lot of experience and wisdom to share. Ask. Don't be afraid. (I know I was and sometimes still am afraid. That's absurd.) Get all the help you can get. Pray that the Lord, your Ultimate Career Coach, puts the right mentor in front of you. And then don't be shy about asking. Be bold and courageous!

Opportunity Knocks (There Are No Coincidences)

How do you know what the right opportunity is? And when will the right door open?

> **"For I know the plans I have for you,"** declares the LORD, **"plans to prosper you and not to harm you, plans to give you hope and a future."** (Jeremiah 29:11 NIV)

> Commit to the LORD whatever you do, and he will establish your plans. (Proverbs 16:3 NIV)

Notice that it's His plans for you. Do you want your plans or His? Without Him, I can do nothing or at least nothing that really matters, matters for eternity. Let Him establish the plans that will "give you hope and a future."

So how do you know what the Lord's plans are for you? Most of us don't know the exact plans the Lord has or when it will appear. The only people who seem to know are those who look back over their lives and then can see what He was doing all along. So we need to continue to keep our eyes and ears open, looking for the next opportunity to present itself. Look for the next step. Again, the Lord knows the plans He has for you. Your job is to trust Him and "not conform to the pattern of this world, but be transformed by the renewing of your mind. Then you will be able to test and approve what God's will is— his good, pleasing and perfect will" (Romans 12:2 NIV).

Assuming you have been praying for your dream job and seeking the Lord's direction, you have asked others to pray as well and you are praying for them, and you have taken your next step by rolling away a stone, any opportunity that presents itself is not a coincidence, even though I don't believe in coincidences. However, not every opportunity is the right opportunity.

So what should you do next? Pray! And then pray some more. Ask the Ultimate Career Coach to confirm this opportunity or ask Him what you need to learn from this experience. It might be that the job sounds perfect and you have the qualifications, but the employer is not someone you have a good feeling about. Pray! Ask your prayer team to pray.

Do your research. Research the company and the leaders. Ask other employees. There is nothing wrong with research. "Test and approve." I believe that God wants us to learn all we can. We need to look at new opportunities from every angle. Test it. Approve or reject. But at some point, we need to trust Him and take a step of faith. It's just like becoming a Christ follower. You learn and research all you can, but at some point, you have to make a decision.

To find the right next step, you might need to knock on several doors and test several doorknobs. However, you are praying that the Lord will open the right door for you. You want His plans because it will be the best for you and your family. If you jump at the first opportunity that presents itself (assuming you already have a job), you might miss the right opportunity. Jesus said, "Ask and it will be given to you; seek and you will find; knock and the door will be opened to you" (Matthew 7:7 NIV).

There is something to learn from every interview. Even if you think the job opportunity doesn't line up with what you think you are looking for, go on the interview. Ask questions. Learn as much as you can. Get as comfortable as you can with the interview process. In fact, the easiest interview is the one where you really don't care that much about the new opportunity.

Some of the best interviews were those that were a definite no. You learn what you don't want and don't like. The more you learn about what is out there, the better your next career decision will be. You might learn that some of your preconceived ideas are all wrong. Use every opportunity as a learning experience. There is something to learn from every conversation. Ask the Lord what He wants you to learn. Be open to listening. Do not shut your mind off. You might just miss Him answering your prayer. Make the most of every opportunity, even if you find out later that it wasn't for you.

> And we know that in all things God works for the good of those who love him, who have been called according to his purpose. (Romans 8:28 NIV)

> Be very careful, then, how you live—not as unwise but as wise, making the most of every opportunity, because the days are evil. Therefore do not be foolish, but understand what the Lord's will is. (Ephesians 5:15–17 NIV)

"All things." All interviews can be used according to His plan for you. Be excited about the opportunity to learn something about others and what they do. You are called to be a light, even in the interview with a stranger. Oh wait, here is an opportunity for you to tell a stranger about yourself. Imagine that. How many people ask you during a normal day to tell them about yourself? It's like you have been given a golden opportunity to witness to them about Jesus. Now, I don't think you should hand an interviewer a religious tract, but I do think you can have a smile on your face, talk well of your previous and current employers, tell them where you go to church and your involvement there, and say you have been praying about this job opportunity. Be positive and happy. Why not? You have Jesus there with you.

How would you answer all the interviewer's questions if you had Jesus sitting in the chair next to you? Before the interview, you should pray that Jesus will be with you, and I believe He will be. So act like it. Be a reflection of His light. I believe people will want to hire you and be around you if you reflect His light. "Rise up; this matter is in your hands. We will support you, so take courage and do it" (Ezra 10:4 NIV).

Balance and Quality of Life (Abundant Life)

When I was growing up, my father always said, "Work hard if you want to get ahead in life." Now my children talk about "qualify of life" or "me time," which I don't ever remember being phrases I had ever heard in my early life. Then there is the phrase "work/life balance." Again, I had never heard that either. Work was what you did to get ahead and then hope you could enjoy your life when you retired. My thoughts and preconceived ideas were all messed up. However, my children's generational thoughts on work/life balance and quality of life are not much better.

I have to ask: What would be the quality of life without Jesus? My life before Jesus was really out of balance, in more ways than just work. And what kind of work/life balance can you have if Jesus is not connecting work and life? These are some of the questions I ask myself. Everything comes back to Jesus. Jesus said, *"A thief is only there to steal and kill and destroy. I came so they can have real and eternal life, more and better life than they ever dreamed of"* (John 10:10 MSG).

What would a *"more and better life"* look like? Doing your best and trusting the Lord for the rest. Jesus didn't die on the cross so we could have a mediocre existence here on earth and then go to Heaven. We are called to be the best and do our best. We are called to be a light, to reflect His love.

What kind of life do you dream of? What if your life turned out better than you could have ever dreamed or imagined? Why wouldn't we trust our Creator that He has the perfect plan for our time here and in Heaven?

I think most of us know when our lives are out of balance. We typically know if our diet, exercise, sleep, TV time, and so forth are not sensible and healthy. And yet we make unhealthy or unbalanced decisions all the time. We need some discipline to keep things in order. Without structure things typically turn into a mess. Nobody I know of likes discipline. Why would we? We want to run our own lives, do what we want to do when we want to, and enjoy what we think will bring us happiness. No parent wants this for their children, so why would we allow this for ourselves? I am not saying we all need to be like marine drill sergeants, but we do need some healthy boundaries.

For me, I have a hard time in certain areas of my life. I tend to be a workaholic and get home after six most every workday. I could do better, but I don't set a healthy boundary. When I get home this late, I'm tired and ready to go to sleep soon, so I don't have much energy to be a good husband and father. Now my work might be excelling, but my home life is suffering. What's the point if the most important thing to me, my family, gets the meager leftovers and suffers. My father, one of my mentors, keeps telling me I need to be home by five every night. I could do this, and I am a pretty disciplined person in other areas of my life, but I can't seem to get this right. I need to set boundaries and stick to my plan. I need discipline in this area of my life.

> Whoever loves discipline loves knowledge, but whoever hates correction is stupid. (Proverbs 12:1 NIV)

> Whoever disregards discipline comes to poverty and shame, but whoever heeds correction is honored. (Proverbs 13:18 NIV)

> Those who disregard discipline despise themselves, but the one who heeds correction gains understanding. (Proverbs 15:32 NIV)

> Listen to advice and accept discipline, and at the end you will be counted among the wise. (Proverbs 19:20 NIV)

> They disciplined us for a little while as they thought best; but God disciplines us for our good, in order that we may share in his holiness. No discipline seems pleasant at the time, but painful. Later on, however, it produces a harvest of righteousness and peace for those who have been trained by it. (Hebrews 12:10–11 NIV)

According to the verses above, discipline leads to knowledge, honor, understanding, and wisdom, which then "produces a harvest of righteousness and peace." But our tendency is to dislike this word and anytime someone says it. Maybe it would help if we replaced the word "discipline" with "being intentional." Discipline sounds like a punishment, but being intentional is deciding up front what we want our outcome to be and then acting on it.

Let's be intentional. Let's decide up front what we want our lives to look like, reflect, and impact. Jesus was intentional more than anyone who has ever walked on this planet. He was intentional about saving the demon-possessed man and the women at the well. He was intentional about mentoring His disciples. He was intentional about dying for us on the cross to pay for our sins. Yet in all His intentionality, He had time for others in need and time for His heavenly Father. He led an intentional and balanced life, yet He had the most important job ever assigned to mankind.

Be intentional about your quality of life. Be intentional about having a balanced life. Be intentional about having time for others in need. But none of this will happen unless you are intentional about your time with our heavenly Father. All of this intentionality will lead to an abundant life. Jesus said so, and I believe Him with all my heart.

Repeat (It's a Journey)

Just because you got your dream job doesn't mean you stop the process. This is not a one-and-done. We should continue to be the best with where we are but always looking for the next opportunity to make a greater eternal impact. Some of the greatest examples in the Bible were made late in life before they made a real impact: Enoch, Noah, Job, Abraham, Moses, Joshua, Daniel, Isiah, and the disciple John.

The Peter Principle is a theory that people advance in their careers to a point where they become incompetent and causing harm. Let's never prescribe to this outcome. We always want to be curious, learn, and have a positive impact. We are called to be a light. Not just today, but always.

You will always be more productive and of value if you keep your resume up to date, pray about your next step, and trust the Lord. Who knows, you could be the next Moses, who started leading a vast number of people at the age of eighty.

Lastly, one of the common comments from previous job seekers when discussing their journey looking for their dream job is that they never felt closer to the Lord. During the searching season, most Christians are genuinely seeking the Lord constantly. They are praying and looking for guidance and direction. Once they get where they want to be, they tend to slack off in their quiet time and intimacy with our Source. And we know this makes no sense, but we act as if we don't need Him for the present moment once we think things are going in the right direction. Please don't let this happen to you.

I recently went to a seminar put on by David Green, the eighty-year-old founder of Hobby Lobby. He had no desire to retire and wanted to work until he couldn't. I don't think he has ever had a burnout phase in his career because he keeps two verses central to all he did and does.

> Rejoice always, pray without ceasing, give thanks in all circumstances; for this is the will of God in Christ Jesus for you. (1 Thessalonians 5:16–18 ESV)

> ... You do not have [direction, guidance, and wisdom] because you do not ask God. When you ask, you do not receive, because you ask with wrong motives, that you may spend what you get on your pleasures. (James 4:2–3 NIV)

What Mr. Green asks for is wisdom in every situation. He prays constantly without ceasing. And lastly, he wants to give thanks to the Lord for everything and then live an extremely generous life. He gets up and goes to work six days most weeks, excited about doing what he does best so he can give God the glory and give away his earnings to missions that will make an eternal impact.

Regardless of age, where you are in your career, and your circumstances, we are back to the biblical principles and the fact that our heavenly Father loves us. Be thankful for today, pray always, and seek Him. Life here on earth will always be exciting with Him by your side, and Heaven will be the best.

APPENDIX A
Parents and Grandparents
(Pray Your Part for Family)

As a parent or grandparent, what is the most important thing you can do for your family? I would argue it is to set an example. So what example are you setting? This is a scary thought for me. Do I lead a life dedicated and trusting in the Lord? Do my actions show I am dependent on Him? What do my children and grandchildren see in me?

If you are like me, you have made many mistakes in raising your children and setting an example. But it is never too late. I think of the two thieves on the cross next to Jesus. Had their families been present, what did they see in their fathers? One was bitter to the end; the other asked for forgiveness and put his trust in Jesus. These two both set examples. I want to be the one who asks for forgiveness and puts his trust in Jesus.

I believe the next best thing a parent can do after setting an example is praying continuously for their family. They need all the protection they can get from the evil one.

> Cast all your anxiety on him [by praying continuously] because he cares for you. Be alert and of sober mind. Your enemy the devil prowls around like a roaring lion looking for someone to devour. (1 Peter 5:7–8 NIV)

There is not a parent I know of who doesn't pray for their children. I believe that even atheists pray for their children. We all want the best for them. So what is the best? The age-old questions are: How do you measure success? By dollars and possessions or by a life of love, purpose, direction, and meaning? Jesus said, *"What good will it be for someone to gain the whole world, yet forfeit their soul? Or what can anyone give in exchange for their soul?"* (Matthew 16:26 NIV).

I think all parents want everything for their children and grandchildren. Parents want them to be successful in the marketplace and lead a life of love, purpose, direction, and meaning, plus free from pain and then spending eternity in Heaven. I suspect we all are praying something like the Prayer of Jabez for each of our children:

> Jabez cried out to the God of Israel, "Oh, that you would bless me [my children] and enlarge my [their] territory! Let your hand be with me [them], and keep me [them] from harm so that I [they] will be free from pain." And God granted his request. (1 Chronicles 4:10 NIV)

This is a great prayer, but when we pray in this fashion and it comes to pass, our children might think that their territory increased by their own ability and strength. If we pray a more focused prayer and when it comes to pass, there is less room to believe that it happened only by their efforts. They will start to realize that the only way it happened was through the power of the Lord and our prayers. I know when the Lord answers my prayers, I know it happened because of divine intervention. The results are that it builds my faith.

Therefore, ask your children and grandchildren how you can specifically pray for them. Ask them what their dream job and career would look like. Ask them to write it down. Then tell them that you will continually pray for this until it happens or they feel their desire has changed in a different direction. So continuously pray as Jesus taught us to.

Then Jesus taught the followers that they should always pray and never lose hope. He used this story to teach them: *"Once there was a judge in a town. He did not care about God. He also did not care what people thought about him. In that same town there was a woman whose husband had died. She came many times to this judge and said, 'There is a man who is doing bad things to me. Give me my rights!' But the judge did not want to help the woman. After a long time, the judge thought to himself, 'I don't care about God. And I don't care about what people think. But this woman is bothering me. If I give her what she wants, then she will leave me alone. But if I don't give her what she wants, she will bother me until I am sick.'"*

The Lord said, *"Listen, there is meaning in what the bad judge said. God's people shout to him night and day, and he will always give them what is right. He will not be slow to answer them. I tell you, God will help his people quickly. But when the Son of Man comes again, will he find people on earth who believe in him?"* (Luke 18:1–8 ETR)

So *"always pray and never lose hope"* because *"he* [God] *will always give them what is right. He will not be slow to answer them. I tell you, God will help his people quickly."* When Jesus *"comes again, will he find people on earth who believe in him?"*

When our prayers are answered, our faith increases, and so does the faith of our children and grandchildren. The ultimate sign of true success is if our children and grandchildren put their faith in Jesus and then live a life of love, purpose, direction, and meaning and ultimately spend eternity in Heaven.

APPENDIX B
Start a Small Group (Be in Community)

Most everyone I know believes they could do more, have more responsibility, make more money, have more influence, and make more of an eternal impact. So you are not alone, so why go alone. Start a small group called "Faith to Find Your Dream Job".

Based on Biblical principals and what we have found, you need others to pray in agreement for your dream job. You also need to bless others by praying for them to get their dream job. Then lastly, you can have others hold you accountable to take your next step as you also help them by being accountable to you about their next step.

We know that small groups are good for you. We need close relationships with others and to feel that we belong to a positive community. My pastor always says, "Real change happens only in the context of relationship with others." And I know you want to change; you want to be all that The Lord has created you to be. The small group setting helps us walk out our faith with others. And I know from personal experience, my faith has grown as I see The Lord answer my prayers for others.

On top of this, I don't know anyone who doesn't need encouragement. You need it as well. So let's be in a group that allows us to be transparent, compassionate, empathetic, and caring. Let's show others love.

I go to a large church, and we are able to register a small group online and then just sit back and see what happens. You will be surprised when people start inquiring about this group because they are in the same rut as you are.

You can go to our website, www.UltimateCareerCoach.com and get your group to download the book for free and find other valuable resources to help you.

You can use the Table of Contents as an outline for what to discuss weekly.

SMALL GROUP OUTLINE:
Week 1: Introduction
Week 2: Write It Down
Week 3: Praying in Agreement
Week 4: Praying and Blessing Others
Week 5: Removing the Stone or Next Steps
Week 6: Looking at the Past
Week 7: Looking at the Past (continued)
Week 8: Reviewing the Present
Week 9: Reviewing the Present (continued)
Week 10: Goals for the Future
Week 11: Goals for the Future (continue)
Week 12: Celebration

One last helpful tip: put all the group's dream job prayer request together and send this to all the members so everyone is praying for the same results. It is also a helpful reminder for them to be praying for their comembers. I know I need all the help I can get in this area because my natural tendency is to think only of myself.

Starting a small group just might be your Next step. Try it. The Lord will surprise you and bless you!

Printed in the United States
by Baker & Taylor Publisher Services